S0-BEA-122

What were the earliest Indians in America like? How did their colorful civilizations develop? What do we know of their cities, inventions, art, studies in astronomy, religion, counting systems, and superstitions? How did proud Indians respond to the first white men they saw?

Answers to these questions and to hundreds more fill the pages of this fast-moving narrative, which tells the wonder-filled story of the American Indians from prehistoric times to the present.

THE AMERICAN INDIAN

SMITHSONIAN INSTITUTI

The AMERICAN INDIAN

Adapted for young readers

by ANNE TERRY WHITE

From the text by William Brandon for

THE AMERICAN HERITAGE BOOK OF INDIANS

Edited by Alvin M. Josephy, Jr.

Introduction by

John F. Kennedy

President of the United States

RANDOM HOUSE NEW YORK

 Manufactured in the United States of America.
Library of Congress Catalog Card Number: 63-7816

Table of Contents

INTRODUCTION

JOHN F. KENNEDY

PRESIDENT OF THE UNITED STATES

For a subject worked and reworked so often in novels, motion pictures, and television, American Indians remain probably the least understood and most misunderstood Americans of us all.

American Indians defy any single description. They were and are far too individualistic. They shared no common language and few common customs. But collectively their history is our history and should be part of our shared and remembered heritage. Yet even their heroes are largely unknown to other Americans, particularly in the eastern states, except perhaps for such figures as Chief Joseph and his Nez Perce warriors of the 1870s, Osceola and his magnificent, betrayed Seminoles of the 1830s, and possibly Sacagawea, the Shoshoni "bird woman" who guided the lost Lewis and Clark expedition through the mountain passes of Montana.

When we forget great contributors to our American history—when we neglect the heroic past of the American Indian—we thereby weaken our own heritage. We need to remember the contributions our forefathers found here and from which they borrowed liberally.

When the Indians controlled the balance of power, the settlers from Europe were forced to consider their views, and to deal with them by treaties and other instruments. The pioneers found that Indians in the Southeast had developed a high civilization with safeguards for ensuring the peace. A northern extension of that civilization, the League of the Iroquois, inspired Benjamin Franklin to copy it in planning the federation of States.

But when the American Indians lost their power, they were placed on reservations, frequently lands which were strange to them, and the rest of the nation turned its attention to other matters.

Our treatment of Indians during that period still affects the national conscience. We have been hampered—by the history of our relationship with the Indians—in our efforts to develop a fair national policy governing present and future treatment of Indians under their special relationship with the Federal government.

Before we can set out on the road to success, we have to know where we are going, and before we can know that we must determine where we have been in the past. It seems a basic requirement to study the history of our Indian people. America has much to learn about the heritage of our American Indians. Only through this study can we as a nation do what must be done if our treatment of the American Indian is not to be marked down for all time as a national disgrace.

THE AMERICAN INDIAN

1. PEOPLE OF THE DAWN

In the first days of men the world was new. It really was, for it had recently been remade. The landscape of marsh and mud over which the giant reptiles trod had been transformed into mountains, streams and forests. Flowers bloomed, birds sang, the earth was rich with color. It was grander and more beautiful than it had ever been before.

But while thousands of generations of ape men and men of the Old Stone Age roamed the Old World, the Western Hemisphere lay untouched. No human eyes took in the beauty through all those hundreds of thousands of years. So we suppose. For even the most ancient human bones found in the Americas are of men like ourselves, bones of Homo sapiens, a creature who appeared on earth possibly 100,000 years ago.

It was at some unknown time after this date that the ancestors of the American Indians entered the still untouched New World. Who were they? Where did they come from?

Wild guesses have been made at various times. Learned men have called the Indians Egyptians, Phoenicians, Greeks, Romans, Chinese, Japanese, Welsh, Irish. Some have urged that the Indians came by way of the lost continent of Atlantis or of Mu, or both. The notion that they were descendants of the Lost Ten Tribes of Israel was once very popular indeed.

Today we know better. Modern science has shown that the American Indians are far older than any of the peoples they were claimed to be. Finds have been made proving that the earliest Americans were here along with camels, mammoths, giant ground sloths, and primitive horses. By the end of the last great Ice Age—which is to say close to 10,000 years ago—men were here positively. And even that far-off date is being pushed back ever further. Carbon 14 tests and other evidence have set men in America back probably to 20,000 years ago, and a recent find near Puebla, Mexico, may push him back to well before 30,000 years ago.

One thing is sure. If the American Indians can claim descent from those early people of 15,000 to 20,000 years ago—and some undoubtedly can—then they are by far the oldest known race on earth. For all the other modern races—Mongolian, Caucasian, and Negro—did not appear till much later.

This means that the first discoverers of America arrived long before there were any boats that could cross an ocean. How, then, did they get over? Where did they enter?

One place immediately suggests itself—Alaska. They could have crossed over from the Old World only by way of Bering Strait, which separates Asia from North America by less than 60 miles. Moreover, two stepping-stone islands—the Diomedes—break the water distance into still shorter hops. And the Strait is at times frozen over and in the past has often been dry land. Add to this the fact that some Indians look very Mongolian and the thing is certain—Alaska was without any doubt the place of entry. The experts agree so entirely that it is

This jade head, carved in Mexico by the Olmecs, calls up America's forgotten past.

scarcely regarded as theory any more, but as a well-established fact.

During the last Ice Age the Arctic coast of Alaska and the Mackenzie River valley were free of ice. Most of Siberia, on the other hand, was icebound. So if the first men did not come in the warm period just before the ice advanced for the fourth and last time, we get a picture of what must have happened. Behind them the ice was slowly smothering Siberia. In front of them the fleeing game was filling up the valleys of Alaska. The Indians followed the game.

They did not stay in Alaska. Though Canada was mainly icebound, for thousands of years during the last advance of the ice, an ice-free corridor ran along the eastern Rockies all the way from the Arctic to the open country south of Canada. Later, other routes may have been open to them. The first discoverers of America trekked on to warmer lands.

They came, just a few at a time, in little knots that looked quite different and spoke different languages. Nobody was in a hurry. People lived for generations in one small area. Great-grandmothers and great-grandsons knew the same hills or plains, rivers or rocks. It seemed to them that they had always lived in the same place. And yet there was movement, very gradual movement. Perhaps it took something like 25,000 years for the Indians to spread from Bering Strait to the tip of South America, to discover the land from the Pacific to the Atlantic.

The manner of that great trek is hidden in the mists of time. But bones and chipped stones tell us bits of the story. Wherever she came from, however she got there, a young woman died some 8,000 or 10,000 years ago in what is now west Texas near the New Mexico line at a site called Midland. Wind scoured the sand away from over her bones and they were found in 1953.

Wherever they came from, however they got there, men lived in Fell's Cave near the southern tip of South America some 8,000 or 10,000 years ago. At about the same time in Nevada, 4,000 miles away, men lived in Gypsum Cave. Both sets seem to have butchered 20-foot ground sloths, which they may have kept penned up like cattle. And both groups left behind stone tools and spearheads.

Several thousand years before this—at least 11,000 or 12,000 years ago—people who hunted mammoths lived on the shores of Ice Age lakes near Clovis, New Mexico. They left ivory spearheads as well as points of stone among the animal bones. Earlier still, people living in the mountains of New Mexico lugged a mammoth tusk into the Sandia Cave that was their home and left it there along with spear points and the bones of camels, mastodons, and prehistoric American horses. Carbon 14 tests say that mammoth tusk is more than 20,000 years old. But the people may not go back so far. The tusk may have been several thousand years old when the Indians got hold of it.

In a "barbecue pit" on Santa Rosa Island off California, the burned bones of pigmy mammoths have been found. They go back some 29,000 years. But there again comes a question. Was the barbecue pit really made by men?

From Siberia, across Bering Strait, the early Americans came. Skirting the ice of the Wisconsin Glacier—shown on the map in white—various groups of them moved down the warm valleys. They spread to the very tip of South America. Some of the important sites where different peoples lived and left traces are noted on the large map and inset.

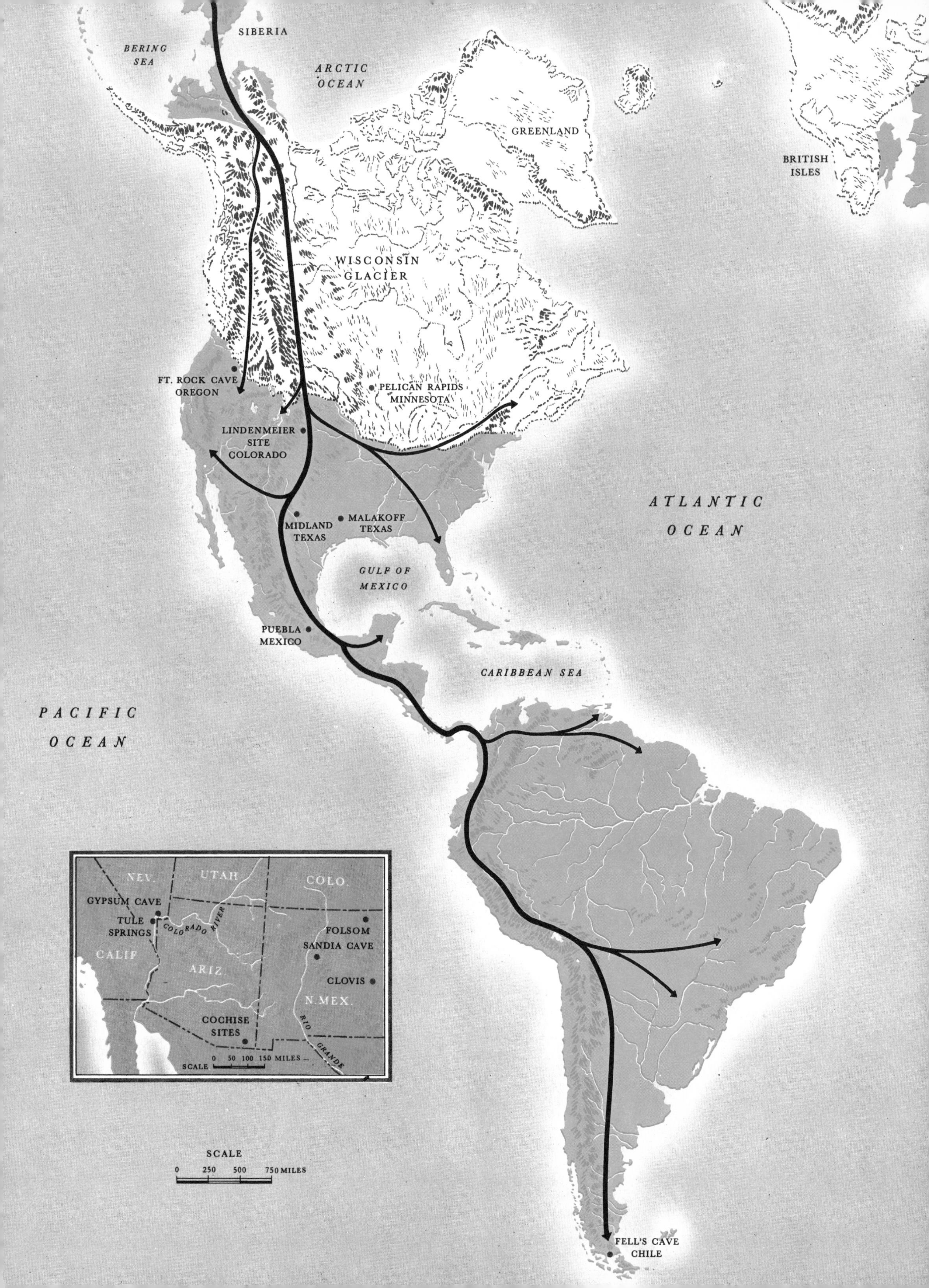

SIBERIA
BERING SEA
ARCTIC OCEAN
GREENLAND
BRITISH ISLES
WISCONSIN GLACIER
FT. ROCK CAVE OREGON
PELICAN RAPIDS MINNESOTA
LINDENMEIER SITE COLORADO
ATLANTIC OCEAN
MIDLAND TEXAS
MALAKOFF TEXAS
GULF OF MEXICO
PUEBLA MEXICO
CARIBBEAN SEA
PACIFIC OCEAN
NEV.
UTAH
COLO.
GYPSUM CAVE
TULE SPRINGS
COLORADO RIVER
FOLSOM
SANDIA CAVE
CALIF.
ARIZ.
CLOVIS
N.MEX.
COCHISE SITES
RIO GRANDE
SCALE 0 50 100 150 MILES
SCALE
0 250 500 750 MILES
FELL'S CAVE CHILE

Perhaps this is how the first Americans saw the Yukon wilderness.

In 1870 near Mexico City a llama bone was dug up from 40 feet under the ground. The bone was carved to represent the face of a wild pig or coyote. The unknown artist who carved that bone lived perhaps 11,000 years ago.

Not far from Dallas, Texas, workers in a gravel pit found three heavy disks of sandstone. It gave the diggers a strange feeling to see crude human faces peering at them out of the stone. Those faces were peering across the past that reaches back to long before the end of the Ice Age.

All these are steps on the long trek. The people of the dawn came long before the bow and arrow were invented. They came perhaps before the dog was domesticated. They had fire, they roasted meat, they worked stone, horn, and bone. Hides, too, most likely. We guess at that because some of the skeletons of the extinct great-horned bison have the tail bones missing. The skins, tail and all, must have been taken to make robes.

The people came. They made the two Americas their own. They were here when Niagara Falls came into being. They were on hand when the top of Mount Mazama in Oregon collapsed and Crater Lake was born. They watched through the long dawn of a new earth.

We picture those watchers only dimly.

DR. J. L. GIDDINGS, JR.

This vast, empty expanse lies between the tall peaks of the St. Elias Range.

We see them standing, leaning on their spears, dreaming through that long, long time—so much longer than all the time of written history—when nothing really changed at all. To us those slow, monotonous centuries seem endless. For us they are punctuated mainly by the changes in the shape of spear points and dart points and, later on, arrowheads.

The people who lived in Sandia Cave perhaps 20,000 years ago left spear points with one shoulder only. The people who hunted mammoths on the shores of vanished lakes near Clovis, New Mexico, more than 10,000 years ago left spearheads about the same size but bullet-shaped, grooved

TEXAS MEMORIAL MUSEUM

Some prehistoric sculptor carved this ancient stone face found near Malakoff, Texas.

GILCREASE INSTITUTE, TULSA, OKLAHOMA

The smallest of these spear points is two inches long. It is a Folsom point of about 10,000 years ago. Just above it is a Clovis point, a crude forerunner, some 2,000 years older. The one-shouldered Sandia points at top and bottom were made perhaps 20,000 years ago. All of them were named after the places in New Mexico where archaeologists first found them.

part way up the face, and without a shoulder.

Some thousands of years later, the famous Folsom point came into use. We call it famous because it proved for the first time how very much longer man had lived in America than anyone supposed. When that point was found, in 1926, embedded between the ribs of an Ice Age bison, it became clear that man and the bison had lived at the same time. A great many Folsoms have since been found in the High Plains east of the Rockies. They are small, light, beautifully made points with a long groove running up each side. Points like that killed many an antique bison with a hornspread of six feet. The Folsom people—so called because the first points were found near Folsom, New Mexico—lived in a borderland time. They were here 9,000 or 10,000 years ago when the Ice Age was dying and the Present was being born.

Stone was not the only thing the Indians used for their points. In the Great Lakes area there was copper. The Indians in and about Wisconsin made lance points and lots of other things out of it. Until a little while ago these copper objects were supposed to be only some 1,200 years old. But they go back to between 5,000 and 7,000 years ago, which is a very early time for using metal anywhere in the world.

Something else punctuates for us that long, uneventful dawn. In the blazing desert country where Arizona, New Mexico, and Mexico meet, there was once a lake to which the name Cochise has been given. Here for many thousands of years lived a people as ancient as the Folsom hunters. But the Cochise people had a different way of life—they were seed gatherers. They left behind them stones and pestles which we call "milling stones" because they were so clearly used for grinding or pounding some sort of wild grains or seeds. Nine thousand years ago is a very early time for pounding seeds into meal.

Perhaps the most exciting early marker is maize. It was found in Bat Cave in western New Mexico. The maize is of a very primitive kind. It is a "pod corn"—each kernel is wrapped up in its own little husk. This is very early corn, but it isn't wild. It was bred by man. And it is some 5,000 to 6,000 years old. Now, corn must have been developed much farther to the south and must have taken a long time to move up to New Mexico. So agriculture must date much farther back than this. Which makes us draw a long breath, for in the Old World the first farming villages go back only to between 5,000 and 7,000 years ago.

From end to end of the two Americas they lived, these hunters and farmers, these many differing groups of many differing kinds of people. Each was a stranger to the rest. They knew about one another only at the fringes, only at the little ripples of contact. But those ripples carried big ideas. They spread ways of life and thought to the farthest points of inhabited land. Sometimes the ideas rippled along exactly as they had rippled in. Sometimes they passed on from group to group all garbled. They started from nowhere and they never ended. They crossed and recrossed each other and the patterns changed and changed.

A man might live out his life and never leave his valley. A family might never have seen foreigners as long as could be remembered. To the individual everything seemed to stand still. But over the long centuries we see the knots of people moving, merging, splitting, multiplying, dying, and appearing from here, there, and everywhere.

We came from beneath the ground, the legends say. We came from the sunrise of the east, or the sunset of the west. We climbed up to the light from the bowels of our holy mountain. We climbed down from the sky by a ladder of arrows.

Each group understood, in its own way, what was around it. Some feared the world and expected evil. Some worshiped its goodness with praise. Some apologized for the animals they killed. Others insulted the beasts they slew. Some were afraid of the dead and fled from them in panic even while weeping with grief. Others hung up the dead in a place of honor in the lodging and kept them there.

But for all the differences, there were remarkable samenesses. All the people, for example, believed in the harmony of things. This harmony was a very shaky thing, however, that could be struck out of balance at any moment. You had to behave just so if you wanted to keep your world steady and avoid such abnormal things as sickness and death.

Two other basic ideas may have been common among early American Indians. Nearly all of them believed in magic power. And nearly all had the idea that land was something that could not be sold. Individuals, families, clans and tribes owned land — but only in the sense that they had the right to *use* it. Land itself was God-given and not a commodity to be sold, any more than the sea or the air.

By the dawn of the period we call the Present, the animal world had changed. The giant beasts of the Ice Age were gone—or nearly; 8,000 years ago the beasts which the hunters had followed had become modern. The native horses were extinct. It was still long before the bow. Men hunted or fought with spears, clubs, slings. They also had bolas—cords weighted at the ends with stones. They would fling the bolas so that they whipped around the animal's legs and tripped it.

We see these people of the long ago Present through a haze. They have no faces. We know some of their weapons and tools, we know bits of their basketry and mats and a few jewels of shell or bone. We can see them making these things. We can see them hunting and fishing, building pitfalls and fish weirs, collecting berries and nuts and roots. We see them moving around. And we guess, from the way they buried their dead, at some of their thinking. But for the most part they elude us. The people of the long ago Present are almost as invisible to us as are the people of the long dawn before them.

2. THE GLORY THAT WAS MAYA

Hunters move around. But crops mean staying close at hand all the time to take care of them. By perhaps 3,500 years ago people began to settle down. There were permanent villages in the Valley of Mexico and in the Guatemala region, where farmers raised both corn and cotton. On the north coast of Peru other village folk cultivated cattails, whose roots are good to eat, chili peppers, squash, gourds, cotton, beans. But not yet corn. There would be no corn in Peru for a long time yet.

All these settled people lived simply and remained very much the same for generations. But in the course of time they began to make pottery. In the Valley of Mexico, sometime around 1350-1100 B.C., there began to appear along with this pottery little clay figurines. And now the people are faceless no longer—we see clearly what they looked like.

They come marching into view tattooed, hung with ornaments, wearing turbans or string hats. Otherwise they are usually naked. Most of them represent women with big hips—the age-old goddess of love. Some of the statuettes are rigid, and yet there is a lot of life locked up in them. Others are

MUSEUM OF THE AMERICAN INDIAN, HEYE FOUNDATION

This tall-hatted pottery figure was probably a powerful warrior-priest of the Mayas. Though recently found on an island off the Yucatan coast, it goes back to A.D. *600 to 900, the Maya Classic Age.*

Catherwood's drawing of a sculptured slab of stone, almost 12 feet high, that was carved by the Mayas at Copan, Honduras.

full of action—they dance and run. They have bewitching smiles and charming bodies. They wear earrings, and their elaborately coiled hair is sometimes streaked red and white. These figurines were very popular—we know that because they were traded all over the valley for many years.

And now a strange thing happens. New ways of doing things come into the Valley of Mexico and to the north coast of Peru about the same time. And along with them come foreign gods. A "feline" or catlike figure is now worshiped in Peru. A jaguar is now worshiped in Mexico.

The strangers who brought the new religion to Mexico about 3,000 years ago have come to be known as the proto-Olmecs. They are called this because they became associated with the part of Mexico where the Olmecs lived 2,000 years later. The proto-Olmecs made the same kind of figurines that had been made before but much better ones and with their own special designs. On nearly everything they touched there was a snarling jaguar's head or else a peculiar "baby face," or something that was monstrous or maimed.

SEATTLE ART MUSEUM, EUGENE FULLER MEMORIAL COLLECTION

This Tarascan warrior, modeled in clay, wears quilted cotton armor and carries a mace. Such armor, the Spaniards found, was superior to their steel breastplates.

The earthenware vessel at the right is in the shape of a dog fattened for the table.

Both clay pieces are from western Mexico.

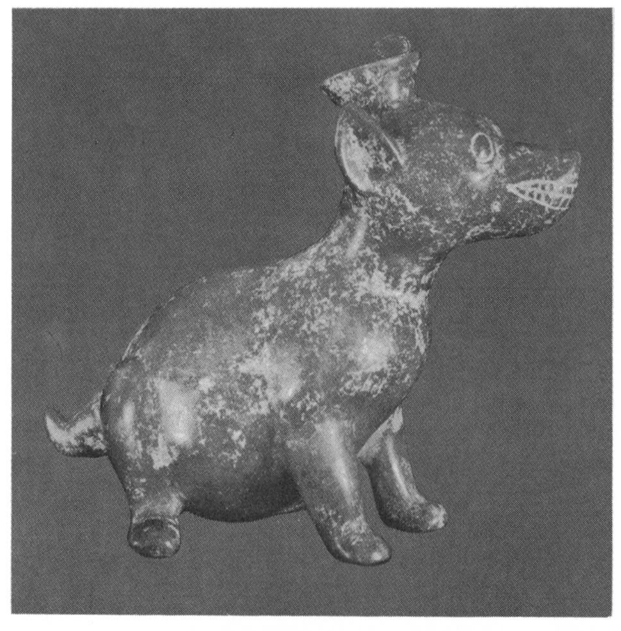

SEATTLE ART MUSEUM, EUGENE FULLER MEMORIAL COLLECTION

MUSEUM OF THE AMERICAN INDIAN, HEYE FOUNDATION

The faces of these figurines were molded, but the rest was made by hand. Village artists of ancient Mexico added tiny clay pellets for eyes, teeth, ear plugs, and headdresses. The dancer and the girl in the swing are both from the Veracruz coast. The pull-toy crocodile shows that the wheel was known in early Mexico.

MUSEUM OF PRIMITIVE ART, NEW YORK

MUSEUM OF THE AMERICAN INDIAN, HEYE FOUNDATION

The map shows important sites in Middle America dating from 1500 B.C. *to* A.D. *1300. Tlatilco and Uaxactun are among the oldest.*

The most important proto-Olmec centers were in southern Veracruz, the rubber country of ancient Mexico. And there on what was their island town of La Venta—which dates from 800 B.C.—amazing things have been found. Archaeologists have unearthed gigantic stone heads up to 14 feet high. The heads glorify the fat-lipped "Olmec" baby face. But what the meaning of these bodyless giants is nobody knows.

While the proto-Olmecs were busy dragging blocks of stone weighing many tons through the mangrove swamps to La Venta and carving them into heads, something much more important was going on in a neighboring land. In the region just next door, to the southeast, other maize-farming people were outgrowing the jaguar and baby-face ideas and creating a style of their own. But they were doing much more than that. They were laying the foundations of a great civilization, one of the highest of the ancient world and the very highest in the two Americas. These people were the Mayas.

We know nearly everything about them. We know how they lived, loved, worked, talked, slept, worshiped, died. We know what they ate and how they cooked it, how they dressed and how they wore their hair (long). We know nearly everything except what they said. And without that we really don't know the Mayas at all. They are the biggest puzzle in American history.

That this should be so is in a way amazing. For the Mayas developed a real written language and some parts of it have been deciphered. Moreover, the people didn't vanish from the earth as so many ancient peoples have done. The Mayas remain, two or three million of them. They speak the various Maya dialects. And in many cases they look so much like their ancestors that it is startling. They could be the pictures on the temple walls come to life. Yet these living Mayas only add to the puzzle. They show us a people that moved not forward but back.

When the Spaniards came to the New World, the Mayas were already well on the way down. But their crumbling world stunned the conquerors. From time to time Spaniards traveled into the jungle and looked at the abandoned "cities" of the Mayas. They couldn't admire enough the beauty of the stone buildings.

"They are so many in number," wrote Diego de Landa, second Bishop of Yucatan, "and so many are the parts of the country where they are found, and so well built are they of cut stone in their fashion, that it fills one with astonishment." To people who hadn't seen them, the Bishop said, "It will seem to be jesting to tell about them."

No one knows the significance of the huge stone heads found at La Venta. BILL AND ILA BROMBERG

That was 400 years ago. But soon after that the wonder died. The last bits of the fading Maya civilization came to an end. Already long before that time, the pyramids, the temples, the "palaces," and other buildings of carved stone had fallen into ruins which the jungle overgrew. And people forgot there had ever been anything but "painted savages" in the Americas.

In 1839 the lost world of the Mayas was found again.

In that year John Lloyd Stephens, a New York lawyer, and Frederick Catherwood, an English architect, traveled into the jungles of Central America to look for themselves at the ruins they had chanced to read about. What they saw thrilled them. When their guide, cutting a way for them with his machete, led them to their first carved stone, they stood in utter amazement before it. It was the figure of a man curiously and richly dressed. The sides of the stone were covered with hieroglyphics.

They stared at it in silence. Then, breathless, they stumbled through the jungle from one carved monument to another. "Savages never carved these stones," Stephens wrote afterwards. This was art, great art. It was a fierce sort of art and one he and Catherwood didn't quite understand, but they recognized that it was art of the highest kind. At Copan, Palenque, and other sites long overgrown with jungle, Catherwood set up his drawing board and copied the intricately carved stones in all their fantastic detail. The mosquitoes were so bad he had to draw with gloves on. But the pictures in stone held him spellbound, and not till the artist fell sick with malaria in June 1840 did the adventure end. The very next year the two friends were back exploring Yucatan.

What a stir there was when the travel books that Stephens wrote came out! Catherwood's pictures went along with the story and helped to arouse tremendous interest in the ruins. History books said there had never been anything but "painted savages" in the Americas. Stephens said he believed that the scattered monuments were all the work of one people and that they were natives of the New World. What is more, they were the ancestors, he believed, of the very Indians who now lived in the region.

For a long time people violently refused to believe that American Indians were capable of such art. But with the help of scholars and archaeologists the Mayas little by little won the credit that was justly theirs.

The so-called cities which they built are not really cities in our sense. It wasn't possible for a farming people to have our kind of towns. And especially because of the way they carried on their farming. To make their cornfields, the Mayas hacked down and burned trees and brush. But as they had no domestic animals which could provide them with fertilizer, their fields soon wore out. Every few years the farmers had to slash out new clearings. Each family had its home in its outlying jungle clearing, and the city was really just a city center to which the people flocked on ceremonial occasions.

We know that there were at least 116 of these ceremonial city centers, scattered over a territory as big as Italy today. Lordly Tikal was the biggest. It might have had a population of 100,000. Little Bonampak had only eleven small buildings. But big or small, a city center was impressive, and it is no wonder Bishop de Landa felt it must be seen to be believed. Clustered at the hub were massive public buildings. Around them stood the so-called palaces or dwellings of the priests and nobles. The temple-topped pyramids dominated the centers,

Maya ruins at Palenque, Mexico, as seen by an artist's eye. Catherwood painted this dramatic view in 1840.

AMERICAN MUSEUM OF NATURAL HISTORY

but there was much else besides. Various centers had bridges, aqueducts, vapor baths. There were monumental stairways, reviewing stands, and plazas for public spectacles. There were astronomical observatories. Some of the more important cities were made up of several clusters of buildings set around separate plazas. They covered many acres and some extended for miles.

Even as ruins these cities of carved stone are breath-taking. Yet they are not the greatest thing the Mayas have left us. Far and away in front are their achievements of the mind. Maya art, Maya mathematics, and Maya astronomy are renowned through the world.

The Mayas had a counting system based not on ten (the fingers of two hands) but on twenty (fingers and toes). Over the years they worked out two systems of figures. One was of dots and bars and would correspond to our Roman numerals, a dot standing for 1 and a bar for 5. Thus 3 bars and 4 dots would equal 19. The other system, of human heads or masks, would correspond to the Arabic. They invented the zero and gave different values to numbers standing in different positions. And they did this 1,000 years before anybody in Europe had a notion of these great ideas.

Their astronomy was just as amazing. They observed the sun and moon so accurately that they could predict eclipses. The Mayas worked out a sun calendar more perfect than ours today. It had 18 months of 20 days each plus one month of 5 days. They counted time so exactly that it came out right to a day within a period of 374,000 years. They also worked out a moon calendar and brought it into relation to their day count with an error of less than 5 minutes a year. They worked out a Venus calendar and meshed it together with their sun calendar. Five Venus years of 584 days each made 8 solar years of 365 days. It was all very complex, wheels within wheels, all turning like a clock, all measuring cycles to the end of time. A cycle of a little less than 20 years was called a *katun*. In what scholars call the Classic Age of the Mayas, which lasted some 600 years, they generally set up a stone monument whenever a *katun* ended. But they did this to mark other cycles too. A cycle of 52 years was the most important one of all.

The more scholars learn about the Mayas

the more they see them wrapped up in timekeeping. Never has there been a people so absorbed in it. And what was it for? There seems to have been very little practical need for all those intricate calculations that took up so much of the priests' time. It seems as if they kept time mainly for the sake of keeping time.

As we have said, the Mayas of today look exactly like their gifted ancestors. But that is only as regards frame and feature. The ancient Mayas tattooed their bodies and painted them—priests blue, warriors black and red, prisoners striped black and white. Sometimes they filed their teeth. They pierced the nose and stuck carved "jewels" in it. They pierced the lobes of their ears and stretched them with ear plugs. They flattened their foreheads and made themselves cross-eyed, a mark of beauty. They decorated themselves with feathers and bred birds in aviaries to provide them with gorgeous plumes. In their hair the men wore brilliant little mirrors of volcanic glass.

The beautiful palaces existed for the pleasure and delight of all, but their specific use was probably reserved for the official activities of priests and nobles. The colorful personal decorations were also just something to look at. The daily lives of the farm folk were extremely simple. A loin cloth sufficed as dress for the men. Families lived in houses of poles roofed with thatch. They tilled their fields, made corn mush, and dangled bits of pitch between a baby's eyes to make him cross-eyed. On the great days they trooped along the straight, well-built roads to the civic centers, where they had their hearts uplifted by a gorgeous spectacle and helped mark another passing point on the holy calendar. Then they went back to their fields. And the nobles acted like aristocrats and sometimes raided each other on state occasions. They read and wrote and studied while the priests gazed over their crossed sticks at the stars. And always and always architects built new temples and craftsmen carved dates on monuments and time turned round and round, never changing.

We can see the Mayas doing all these things, but we don't really know them. We don't because, except for their numbers and the names of their months and a few such things, we can't read what they said. And in any case, save for a few mangled scraps, their books are gone. For the Spanish priests took care to burn—as works of the devil—all the books of history and science, all the lives of great men, the legends and the fables and songs which we know the Mayas had. In the museums of Europe are three Maya books, brought home probably by Spanish soldiers. They look very much like a paper painted on both sides and folded in accordion pleats. A great many of the Maya hieroglyphic signs were in the form of faces of one sort or another.

It seems to us, from what we know, that life went along very smoothly for the Mayas between A.D. 60 when they set up their oldest dated monument, and the time 600 or so years later when they began to fade out. We don't know what happened then to bring the curtain down. All we know is that they began to abandon their cities. Within a century or two all the towering civic centers of this region were deserted.

We shall meet the Mayas again, but not as they were in this, their Classic Age. They seem to us to have been a people lost in thought, a people about whom everything is a puzzle.

"Go and read it and you will understand," says the Jaguar Priest.

But we can't. It's gone.

This mural at Bonampak shows a Maya ceremonial parade of more than 1,000 years ago.

3. FARMERS, PEOPLE OF THE WOOD AND GODS

The Mayas were so creative that they have been called "Greeks of the New World." But they were not necessarily the first people to build pyramids and crown them with temples. Their art in carved wood and stone, in stucco modeling and painting, is the finest in the New World and some of the finest anywhere. But they may not have been the first among their neighbors to practice it. The zero does seem to have been their very own. So does the corbeled vault which they used in building—they didn't know the secret of the keystone arch. But they may not even have been the inventors of their famous calendar mathematics.

In a way the Mayas remind us of the proto-Olmecs—they did many of the same things that were done by others around them, only they did them better. It would be wrong to get the idea that only barbarians surrounded them. Mayaland was the heartland. But all around it little towns and cities were springing up. Corn farming and all the new things that went with it—new gods, new wealth, new ways, new worries—had spread far beyond the Mayas.

To be sure, not all the people of the Maya world were settled farmers. Everywhere beyond the belts of little planted fields were the wandering tribes. Everywhere throughout the boundless areas around the cities, the hunters lived as they always had. To the farmers they were "people of the wood." They were tribes whose faces the farmers did not see, who had no settled homes, who only wandered through the woodlands.

Very far removed from the Mayas in ways and ideas were the people of the wood. Not so the settled farmers in all the middle zone of the Americas, from central Mexico south to Bolivia and Peru.

West along the Gulf Coast from the Maya country were the fat-faced proto-Olmecs and their old, faded city of La Venta. Next door beyond stood Tajin of the Totonacs, a town with a great pyramid and many temples. In the mountaintop cities of the Oaxaca region lived the Zapotecs, who traded their handsome incense burners far and wide. At Cholula in the state of Puebla stood a pyramid bigger than the Great Pyramid of Egypt.

The buildings in central Mexico were less elegant than those of the Mayas, but they made up for that in size. The city of Teotihuacan was one solid procession of grand public buildings and priests' dwellings, all decorated with serpents, beasts, and feathered men of heaven. There was a Temple of the Moon, a Temple of

BILL AND ILA BROMBERG

Tajin's Temple of Niches near Veracruz is Totonac architecture. A mound of earth was faced with stone to make a seven-tiered pyramid. Idols once stood in the niches.

Quetzalcoatl, and the tremendous Pyramid of the Sun. All these buildings and their plazas, parks, and avenues covered a paved area more than three miles long and nearly two miles wide. Teotihuacan—the place "where the gods reside."

All the sprouting cities of Mexico learned to count time as the Mayas did. All of them adopted some form or other of the calendar system that, like the two-headed serpent, swallowed itself every 52 years. The Indians seem to have been fascinated by the idea that everything came to an end and yet was reborn, everything changed and yet stayed the same.

Strangely, the sacrifice of human beings was related to this idea. The Indians didn't sacrifice to appease angry gods. Angry gods are shepherds' gods, gods that live in the lightning. And the Indians kept no flocks. The gods of Teotihuacan were in the sunlight, were in the stars. The Indian gods were hungry, not angry, hungry for the destruction of living things—of men, dogs, birds, flowers, anything that lived—hungry for the death that brought new life. The idea was that without constant death the life of the gods grew weak. Death was the

FRITZ HENLE, PHOTO RESEARCHERS

The Temple of Quetzalcoatl at Teotihuacan is a picture in stone, as this detail shows. The fanged heads represent the feathered serpent that gave the temple its name. The owlish figures may represent the Rain God.

food of the gods.

Teotihuacan was rebuilt twice. The rooms were filled in and the buildings were covered with cut stone and adobe to make platforms for larger buildings. Temples were usually enlarged or rebuilt at the close of every 52-year cycle. But this rebuilding of the whole city was something exceptional. It must have been done for some other reason, and it isn't hard to guess what. Religion and politics went hand in hand. Very likely a new administration came in. Very likely the party of the old gods was overthrown and the party of the new gods raised new temples and made a clean sweep of everything else.

But the old gods never really disappeared. Tlaloc, the Rain God, who was defeated at Teotihuacan, had been a new god once. Yet he had the teeth of the jaguar that had been a god before him. And when he was overthrown, he wasn't cast aside. With some new qualities added, he appeared again. And he remained forever in the front rank of the gods. Quetzalcoatl, a god who was known to many of the Indian peoples as the Plumed Serpent, as God of the Morning, the Bearded Man, Lord of Life, Lord of the Wind, Bringer of Civilization, and so on, lost his temple. It was completely covered over and turned into the foundation for a new building. Still, he continued as a star actor for hundreds of years. The old gods melted into the new. The new gods became other faces for the old.

FRITZ HENLE, PHOTO RESEARCHERS

One mile north of the Temple of Quetzalcoatl at Teotihuacan, the massive Pyramid of the Sun thrusts toward the sky. Although it covers an area about equal to that of Cheop's great pyramid, it has less bulk than the Egyptian tomb.

JOHN LEWIS STAGE, PHOTO RESEARCHERS

4. THE TOLTECS

In the centuries that followed A.D. 600, there was great unrest among the city-states of central southern Mexico, and the Classic Age was pulled to pieces. The Olmecs and the Totonacs left their Veracruz coast and went raging inland, fighting anyone who got in their way. The Zapotecs left their mountaintop city, Monte Alban. A number of towns and cities in Mexico were abandoned too, just as the Mayas were abandoning their jungle centers.

What was behind it all? Famine, disease, or signs and portents in the skies? Nobody knows. All we know is that things went on badly for centuries.

Perhaps the people of the wood who invaded Mexico's cities during this age of unrest may have started the trouble. But then, why were the centuries before the turmoil and after it so stable? There always had been invasions of the wild tribes. For they were always splitting and dividing and going off here, there, and in all directions. They had to. A hunting people can't be very numerous—their hunting grounds can support only so many people. Probably when the splits and divisions came, they weren't peaceful. Those who had to leave the old haunts most likely went forth in anger. Certainly they went forth in grief, doomed to wandering and exile.

A great history lay ahead for one such people, driven out from their homeland on Mexico's Pacific Coast. They were the Toltecs. We know that sometime in the 8th or 9th century, A.D., they came down into the Valley of Mexico. They looted and burned Teotihuacan the magnificent, where stood the great Temple of the Sun. Some of the defeated people helped the Toltecs build their capital city, Tula, north of Lake Texcoco.

These 15-foot Toltec figures were carved in sections and fitted together. Once they supported a temple roof at imperial Tula.

The wandering Toltecs settled down and founded the first real empire in the New World. Before A.D. 1000 they had conquered right to the heart of the Maya country in Guatemala and Yucatan. The Mayas had been quite disorganized after they abandoned their cities and moved to Yucatan. But now, instead of being crushed, they had a wonderful rebirth. It was under the Toltecs that they built their beautiful Chichen Itza, the shining city which archaeologists have dug out of the ruins. Chichen Itza is new-style Maya. The Toltec influence is very clear to see at Chichen Itza.

The Toltecs were no longer rude barbarians—all that was behind. They had taken in the civilization they found and had added new and brilliant ideas. Their buildings are full of grace and power. The peoples they conquered looked upon them as geniuses whose style in building and carving and painting it might be well to copy. For centuries after the Toltec empire was no more, ruling families proudly insisted they were descended from the Toltecs.

Tradition says it was the Toltecs who

BIBLIOTHEQUE NATIONALE, PARIS

Rival gods from Aztec picture manuscripts. Top, gentle Quetzalcoatl, the Morning Star. Bottom, black Tezcatlipoca, Lord of the Night, who warred against Quetzalcoatl.

BIBLIOTECA APOSTOLICA VATICANA, VATICAN CITY

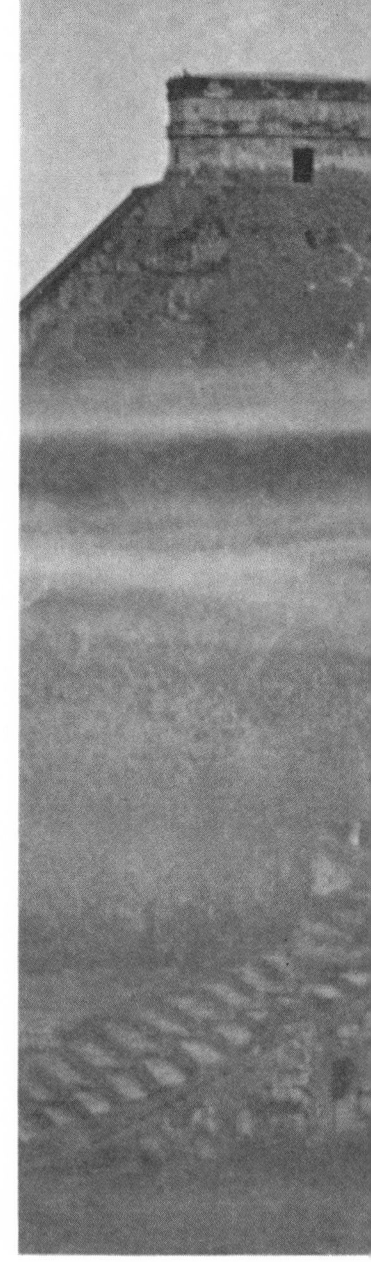
NORMAN CARVER

Chichen Itza in Yucatan, indicative of the second stage of Mayan civilization, is a showplace today. Archaeologists dug it out of the ruins. In this picture Castillo, *the great pyramid of Kukulcan, and the 41-foot-high "observatory" rise through the morning mist. Inside the tower is a circular staircase (which gives the building its Spanish name* Caracol*) leading to a room whose walls were slotted to enable astronomers to observe the stars.*

introduced human sacrifice to the Mayas and brought to Mexico the black god Tezcatlipoca, Lord of the Night, to war with the white god Quetzalcoatl, the Morning Star. Tradition says they also brought to Mexico the sacred ball game, at which the whole audience bet and won and lost everything they owned, from their lip jewels to their lives.

But human sacrifice wasn't new. No one knows when it began. No one can guess who started the practices of sending dead souls to help the sun in his war against the stars and feeding the rain with blood. Nor was the black god Tezcatlipoca, whose symbol was a jaguar skin, new either. For centuries before the Toltecs came, he had been pictured on temple walls fighting the sun. And surely the ball game in which players, without using their hands, tried to knock a solid rubber ball through a vertical ring set 24 feet up in the wall of the ball court, is believed to be very ancient indeed.

Tradition has a great deal to say about the Toltecs. It tells us that their most glorious king was Topiltzin. He was born on the day in their calendar called Ce Acatl (Say Ah-Cattl, One Reed), and so he was given this name too. And since he was educated as a priest of Quetzalcoatl, he got the god's name too for good measure. A wicked uncle had seized his father's throne, but when the boy grew up he killed his uncle and took the kingdom back and ruled with unequaled goodness and wisdom.

So far it all seems possible. Then the impossible begins — Ce Acatl Topiltzin Quetzalcoatl dissolves into Quetzalcoatl the god.

Tradition says the black god Tezcatlipoca appeared on earth and drove Topiltzin from Tula to Cholula and then to Yucatan. Everywhere he was looked on as a saint. He taught people the road of virtue by word and deed. Then he departed to the East and said that in time to come, in the year of Ce Acatl, he would return.

Quetzalcoatl, Feathered Serpent, was the Maya god Kukulcan. After this time he was worshiped in the Maya country as a powerful god. At Chichen Itza the great pyramid and temple are his.

Perhaps there really is some truth at the bottom of the Quetzalcoatl story. Perhaps the greatest Toltec king really was Topiltzin. It was in his time that metalworking, especially in gold, was introduced. And trade grew enormously then. All sorts of wares traveled the roads in the tumpline packs which slaves carried on their backs— everything from macaw feathers and jaguar skins to drinking tubes and chewing gum.

Some areas exported salt, rubber, and dogs fattened for the table. Cacao for the delicious foaming chocolate was so much in demand that cacao beans were used as money. Other regions made a specialty of yarn and embroidered cotton cloth. War clubs with inset sword-blade edges of volcanic glass were articles of trade. So were rope, and carved jade, and turquoise, flutes and tobacco pipes of clay. Pottery, paper, paints, and dyes traveled in the packs.

Some trade went by sea. The Mayas imported at this time the famed Orange pottery from Veracruz. It had to travel more than 600 miles by seagoing canoe. The Mayas carried on a sea trade, too. Maya dugouts with a crew of as many as 25 paddlers carried lime, clay, sapodilla wood hard as metal, corn and vanilla, wax and honey, stone knives, razors, and hatchets. But their chief ware was spun cotton in brilliant colors.

In this period the bright sun that was Mexico cast its beams very far. By around A.D. 1000 the growing of corn and squash

The gleaming Temple of Warriors at Chichen Itza, built in the 12th century, shows how the Toltecs influenced Mayan architecture. NORMAN CARVER

and beans, and the art of making pottery that went along with it, had seeped and trickled here and there throughout nearly all North America, wherever the climate allowed, except the far west coast. Other ideas traveled north too. The descendants of the Cochise people were building ball courts for the sacred game in their irrigated Arizona desert. In the colorful canyons of the country where New Mexico, Arizona, Utah, and Colorado join, the rays of the sun were strongest of all. Here the Golden Age of the Pueblos was dawning. A busy trade with Mexico went on. Live parrots were carried here at least 1,200 miles from the markets of Mexico.

East of the Mississippi was another far frontier of the great Mexican civilization. From the Gulf Coast to Wisconsin, from New York to Kansas and Nebraska, lived prosperous little nations. Many of them built earthwork walls and mounds. Some of these were burial monuments, others were fortifications, altars, or platforms for temples. Things which archaeologists have taken from the mounds show clearly that there was trade with the far south. Some of the items have a distinctly Maya style about them.

Ideas traveled north to the most distant peoples of the woods as well as to the settled farmers. In the northern forests Indians worshiped Quetzalcoatl, transformed into Morning Star. But ideas were going the other way too. The bow was traveling south. Moccasins were traveling south.

GEORGE HOLTON PHOTO RESEARCHE

5. POTTERS, WEAVERS, EMPIRE BUILDERS

Strangely, the rays of the bright sun that went so far north don't seem to have traveled far south. It is true that Mexico and Peru did many of the same things. Both had intensive farming and irrigation, both built ceremonial city centers, temple mounds, and step pyramids. In each society there were classes with kings, and later priest-kings, at the top. And so on down through a long list. In their early ages both even shared some of the very same pottery styles and some similar religious ideas—the jaguar-feline cult. But there were also some very important time lags and differences.

Metal-working was known in the Andean region 1,000 years before it reached Mexican America. If there was any contact to speak of, what took so long? The calendar that spread so far through Mexican America never got to the Andes at all. It may be possible, of course, that the Andeans simply weren't interested in the calendar. But what about corn? Surely they would have wanted corn. Very much. Yet corn had been cultivated in the Mexican area for a very long time before it reached Peru. When corn at last appeared, farming had been going on in the Andean region for 1,000 years.

The lofty Inca fortress-city Machu Picchu remained hidden from the world for centuries. In 1911 it was discovered by Hiram Bingham. Now modern roads bring tourists to wonder at its marvels of perfectly fitted stonework.

Such facts don't argue for close contact. Nor for the idea that the two cultures sprang from the same root and then grew apart.

Most of the specific things that are the same for both Mexico and Peru stem from a single period. This is the period of the jaguar cult in Mexico and the feline cult on the coast of Peru. Perhaps there was communication between the two worlds then. But certainly before this period and after it, any contact was extremely hazy and matter-of-chance. Peru went along on its own.

In 1000 B.C. little farming villages dotted the north coast and the neighboring highlands. Andean farmers had squash, gourds, beans, cotton, and manioc to work with. Corn had just been introduced, and peanuts and avocados. Probably it was at this time that the llama was domesticated. The people wove cloth and did some metal work in sheet gold. Each village was more or less independent of the others, but the people met at the religious centers, where temples stood atop platforms. Chavin de Huantar was a famous center in this age. It was in a little valley near the river Maranon. a modest little stream that gives no hint of being the headwater of the mighty Amazon.

This was the great schooling time in the Andes. Now was the time when the people learned to build in stone. They learned irrigation. They learned how to terrace the

MARC AND EVELYNE BERNHEIM, PHOTO RESEARCHERS

Having little farm land, the Peruvians built terraces on the steep mountainsides. Canals brought water to them, often from miles away.

bare mountainsides to make farmland where there was none. They learned to use guano—bird droppings from the coast—to fertilize their land. They learned all these things so well that through all later Andean times they never needed to be changed. The manner of working the soil with digging stick and hoe was established at this time—the plow would never be known in Indian America. The manner of making pottery was fixed—the potter's wheel would never be invented in the New World.

When a thousand years had passed, a change did come, however. The feline god whom the Andeans had been worshiping sank from sight and the style of art which featured him went out. Slowly, with much hard work, new styles of life grew up in half a dozen different regions. Around A.D. 800-1000 they burst into flower.

Experts marvel at this flowering time, the Andean Classic Age. They talk about the remains of this great period in the same way they talk about Maya art and architecture, only more so. And what the Andean people created at this time really is beyond belief.

Think of what terracing the Andes means, the labor it represents! To make a terrace on the steep, bare canyon sides, the Indians had to carry up on their backs the stones that had rolled down into the valleys. They set these stones up into great retain ing walls, then filled in the space behind with more stones to make a level bed. On top of this they spread soil, every basketload of which had to be carried up on their backs. And they made not one such hanging-garden bed but thousands. Tier upon tier the terraces climbed the mountainsides almost to the top. Irrigation brought water to the farms in spouting jets and trickles that went down from step to giant step. There are terraces in other lands. But there are none like these.

The irrigation canals that ran for miles, the wide roads, the suspension bridges, the huge stone fortresses and ceremonial centers, the houses of stone and adobe, the underground galleries lined with stone, the skilled work in metals—all these the experts marvel at. But what amazes them above all is the pottery and the weaving. So much has been said about them that the people who made them have almost been buried under the mountain of words. Their works live, but they themselves are shadows.

That is, all but the Mochica, the coast people from the Moche, Viru, and neighboring valleys. We can picture them very well because their pottery is full of portraits and caricatures of themselves. It shows every detail of their lives. The pots are like thousands of motion pictures modeled in clay; they are like bits taken out of a television comedy. Many represent scenes of everyday life that anyone can recognize, and many are comical. But there is also much that is dark. Helmeted warriors lope home carrying trophy heads. Captives are sacrificed by being hurled off cliffs. Executioners calmly cut off a convict's lips.

As for the weaving in this flowering time, all the experts agree that the textiles made by the Paracas and Nazca people of the Peruvian south coast are the greatest ever produced anywhere.

The Paracas did almost every kind of weaving we know today. Indeed, modern man hasn't yet matched the best of their work or been able to copy all of their intricate weaves. They made everything from gauze and lace to brocade and tapestry in every sort of color. Archaeologists who have studied the colors say the Paracas weavers used 190 hues in seven color ranges.

This people, whose civilization goes back to 300 B.C., lived where a low line of barren hills juts into the Pacific. Once in a while a wind shifts the hot red sands and reveals a bit more of a secret that was well kept for over 2,000 years. Here in the burial ground of this forgotten people, bodies were discovered wrapped in huge mummy bundles of dazzling white muslins and richly embroidered brocades. It seems the Paracas people were skilled weavers even long before the Andean Classic Age and they used their very best textiles as clothing for the dead.

Medicine was another art in which the Andeans were well advanced. And particularly surgery. One operation they performed over and over—they cut a great hole in the skull, something that surgeons today

VICTOR W. VON HAGEN

Mochica pottery lets us glimpse a people of the northern Peruvian coast 1,000 years ago. This pitcher shows a man clubbing another.

do with hesitation, and only when they cannot avoid it. Yet a great many trepanned skulls have been found in Peruvian graves, and the healing shows that most of the patients got better. Probably the popular weapon of those times—a club with a heavy stone end—was responsible for all those operations. That club must have cracked many a skull and caused pressure on the brain.

Doubtless chewing coca leaves deadened the pain. For coca, from which we get cocaine, had by this time come into use along with many other new things. The white potato, the sweet potato, quinoa, and pineapple were now part of Andean life. Llamas, alpacas, ducks, and guinea pigs were being raised. A beer, *chicha,* was fermented from corn or fruit. Feathered masks, and musical instruments from tambourines to coiled trumpets, were being used in the dances. Balsa boats, large and small, traveled the waters. In fact, everything by now had been created that the Andean world was to have, except really widespread conquest and empire.

That came along in due course.

We don't know too much about it. It crept down from the central Andes, from the region of sky-high Lake Titicaca, and it came in a tide. Most of the little kingdoms were conquered, then united in one realm by about A.D. 1200.

The union didn't last, though. After a century or two or three, this empire fell apart—only to be brought together again by the famous Incas.

The Incas were a tribe of farmers and llama herders in a small way who had once lived on a high plain of the Andes. They made their way north to the valley of Cuzco and overcame its inhabitants. Then one by one they conquered the little kingdoms around them. By 1200 they were a big power. By the year 1492 they had an empire that stretched from northern Ecuador to central Chile and covered a large part of South America.

Once they had things well in hand, the Incas took pains to blot out all the history before their time. They also wiped out their own and spread a myth that changed them into Children of the Sun and benefactors of mankind. They were not an original people like the Mayas. They brought nothing new with them and they invented nothing. Everything they built was copied from the older civilizations they had conquered. In their cities, fortresses, roads, terraces, temples, they did only what had been done before them—but a great deal more of it. Their art never came up to the best work of earlier times, but their output was tremendous.

Only their political organization was their own. They were totalitarians, no mistake about that. If they couldn't trust a conquered nation, they would transplant the whole population to a region where it could be more easily kept in hand. They shunted tribes about like pieces on a chess-

Inca fortress near Cuzco. Some of these snugly fitted stone blocks weigh 200 tons.

VIRGINIE SHELDON

Detail from a Paracas embroidery, with cat design. The best work of the Andean weavers has never been matched.

board. They regulated everything and everybody. They took a census and decided who should do what and for how long. They said what should be made and how much of it. And the workers produced so much that every family in that vast empire had a house to live in and food to eat and clothes to wear.

Naturally the Incas were the aristocracy and had the highest jobs. As for the king, he was absolute, and the splendor in which he lived was truly magnificent. He had 200 palaces filled with riches. The walls of those palaces were covered with gold and silver studded with jewels. He had whole gardens of artificial plants. Their stems, leaves, flowers, and fruit were made of gold and silver. In his perfectly organized empire there was the greatest collection of art in gold and silver the world has ever known.

The emperor was divine, and so, of course, was the head of the church. But the Incas weren't interested in sacrifice. They never got involved with the idea that public death was food for the gods. They had more practical things to do. Still, they took religion seriously. There were countless priests and priestesses housed in countless temples and convents. The Incas worshiped the creator Viracocha, who had made the world and taught all goodness and virtue. They worshiped the Sun and the Thunder. Holy things, like the tombs of the ancestors and especially the bodies of dead emperors, called for sacred ceremonies. Yet the highest point was the simple ceremony in which the emperor offered a cup of wine to the Sun.

The Inca world went along smoothly. The farmers worked the fields, the herders herded the llamas, the miners brought up gold and silver, the engineers built astonishing roads and bridges, and the priests chanted while the elegant Inca gentlemen took snuff. It seemed as if things would continue like that forever.

MUSEO NACIONAL DE ANTROPOLOGIA; FRITZ HENLE, PHOTO RESEARCHERS

6. THE AZTECS

Up in Mexico the Toltec empire had long ago caved in. Savage bowmen from the north had seized, sacked, and destroyed everything in sight. Then they had rebuilt and ruled some of the city-states. Around Lake Texcoco the cities were bigger and richer with gods than ever.

About the middle of the 13th century there wandered into the Valley of Mexico a rude tribe of spearmen who called themselves the Mexica. They hired themselves out as mercenaries at first and, having no land of their own, settled on a miserable little group of islands in Lake Texcoco. They named their dwelling place Tenochtitlan (Place of the Cactus-in-the-Rock).

They prospered. Little by little their town grew. Their chief married a king's daughter, and Tenochtitlan thereupon became a full-fledged city-state. When a hundred years had passed, it was one of the two chief cities in the entire country.

By this time the people no longer called themselves Mexica. They had invented a suitable history and were now Aztecs, for their legends said their original home had been a place called Aztlan. They had also chosen for their very own a suitable god—Huitzilopochtli (Weet-seel-o-poch-tlee), "omen of evil, creator of war." It was this god who had told them to wander until they came to a cactus growing from a rock, on which an eagle would be perched, holding in his beak a serpent. They had found this

The face of an Aztec Eagle Knight, 14 inches high and carved of basalt.

RARE BOOK DIVISION, NEW YORK PUBLIC LIBRARY: LOUBAT COPY

Huitzilopochtli, the Aztecs' bloodthirsty god.

promised land, cactus, eagle, snake and all, exactly as the god had predicted, at the site of Tenochtitlan. Huitzilopochtli had also told them they were his chosen people and would rule the world. The Aztecs proceeded to do so, so far as Mexico was concerned.

Their conquests went on and on, far to the north and south. Tribute and captives poured into the city, and Tenochtitlan grew and grew. Swampland was reclaimed, blocks of new buildings were raised, a three-mile-long aqueduct was built, then another. A thousand people were employed each day just to wash down the streets. Some 300,000 people lived in the city, which became the center of power and wealth for all Mexico.

By the year 1492 there were only a couple of peoples the Aztecs hadn't crushed. Nearly all the rest of Mexico paid them tribute, but the subject peoples often had to be reconquered because the Aztecs didn't try to build an empire in the Inca fashion. For them war had just two aims—to get tribute and to get captives. The captives were for sacrifice. There never were enough to feed the gods, not even with all the wars. So artificial wars—Wars of the Flowers as they were called—were arranged between neighboring cities for the sole purpose of capturing victims from each other. Each side fought until enough prisoners had been taken to satisfy its gods. Then all parted friends, with no hard feelings. So they say.

And still there weren't victims enough. Anyone in Mexico who was ill and needed some god's help bought a slave and on the god's feast day had him slain. The priests needed victims for the temple rites. Military organizations needed victims for their special rites. In the case of the Aztecs, the state constantly needed victims for Huitzilopochtli, who fought each day against the moon and the stars, against the darkness of night. Without blood and human hearts to eat, the sun would fail.

Each of the eighteen 20-day months of the year had its sacrifices. Hearts were torn out for Huitzilopochtli and, at Tenochtitlan, the heads of the victims were stuck on the towering skull rack in the central plaza. Captive warriors were tied to a stone and given mock weapons to fight warriors truly armed. When the hearts had been torn out, priests danced with the heads of the captives.

So many victims were required! It took two years of campaigning to round up enough for the dedication of the great new temple to Huitzilopochtli. How many people were sacrificed on that occasion we do not know, but that the number was staggering is certain.

In 1502 Montezuma came to the throne. It was a time of signs and portents that greatly troubled the young king.

A temple burst into flame without cause and burned to the ground. Another temple was struck down by lightning out of a clear sky. A comet fell in broad daylight, and for four years a column of fire appeared each

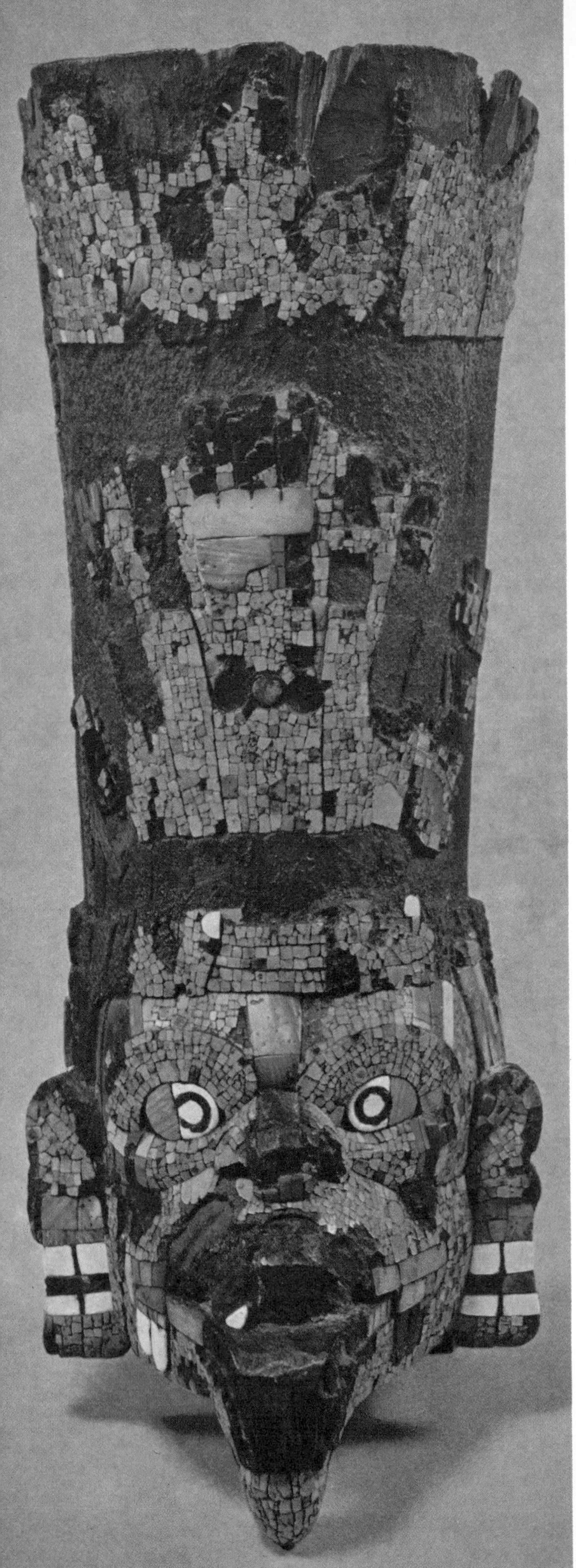

night. A marvelous bird was brought to Montezuma, a crane with a mirror in its head. In the mirror could be seen people coming as conquerors, dressed for war. Deer bore them upon their backs.

Christopher Columbus, or Christ-bearing Dove as we would translate his name if he were an Indian, wrote home a glowing account of what he found in the New World. Especially he was struck with the goodness of the people. "They are artless and generous with what they have," he wrote, "to such a degree as no one would believe but he who had seen it. Of anything they have, if it be asked for, they never say no, but do rather invite the person to accept it, and show as much lovingness as though they would give their hearts."

Then he went on to say they believed very firmly that he, with his ships and crew, came from the sky. "To this day," he said, "I carry them who are still of the opinion that I come from heaven. . . . And they were the first to proclaim it wherever I arrived; and the others went running from house to house and to the neighboring villages, with loud cries of 'Come! Come to see the people from heaven!' "

In 1493 Columbus came a second time to the New World. This time he came with 17 ships and 1,500 people, most of them colonists. He attacked the cannibal Caribs wherever he found them. But he did his best to force the Spaniards to deal justly with the Tainos, as the simple Arawak island people called themselves. "With fifty men they could all be subjected and made to do all that one wished," he wrote in his journal. But he also said, "I knew that they were a people who could better be freed and converted to our Holy Faith by love than by force . . . they remained so much

NATIONAL MUSEUM, COPENHAGEN

The owlish eyes and jaguar fangs of this dazzling mask are those of Tlaloc, the Rain God.

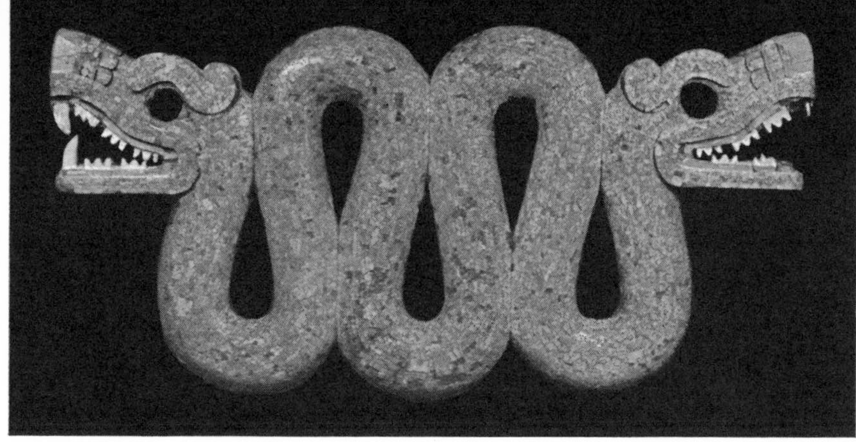

BRITISH MUSEUM

Aztec shell-and-turquoise breast ornament, 17½ inches long. Perhaps this is one of Huitzilopochtli's fire serpents. This god fed on the blood of human sacrifices and his hunger was never satisfied.

our friends that it was a marvel."

But the Spanish settlers needed laborers for their plantations and mines, and the Indians weren't interested in work. Moreover, the priests protested the Indians couldn't be converted unless they were forced into congregations. So when more and more settlers came, it became necessary, of course, to congregate the Indians in villages under Spanish rule and see that they stayed congregated, and worked and worshiped properly.

Some of the Tainos tried to rebel. More fled. More still died from the strange new diseases that had come with the people from heaven. By 1513 there were 14,000 Tainos left out of an original 250,000 or so.

Through all these years the Spaniards never heard of the golden cities of the Aztec and Inca empires. But it would not be long now.

In the year 1511 a Spanish ship struck a reef and sank in the Caribbean. Some of the Spaniards got to the east coast of Yucatan where, ragged and starving, they were found by the Indians. A number were killed, others died in slavery. Only two were left—Aguilar and Guerrero. They were made slaves of Maya chieftains.

At about the same time, far up the Nahua coast of Mexico, a little Indian girl named Malinal was stolen and sold into slavery. She passed from hand to hand and finally found herself on the frontier of the Maya country.

Yucatan was a very different sort of land now. Chichen Itza was no more—war, hurricane, and pestilence had swept over the Mayas. Then in 1516 an epidemic of smallpox struck them. The following year a Spanish ship, hunting slaves, touched on the Yucatan coast not far from where the slave girl Malinal was living. The Mayas drove the Spaniards away in a hot fight. However, the Spanish ships came a second time and a third. The last time they brought 16 horses. The Indians had never seen a horse before. They fled in terror. And this time the Spaniards stayed—and heard about wondrous Tenochtitlan.

The Spanish captain was a young man named Hernando Cortes. He had been told a tale of bearded men in the Maya town, and he got a message through to Aguilar and ransomed him from slavery. But Guerrero would not be ransomed. "I am married and have three children," he said, "and the Indians look upon me as a Cacique and captain in wartime. . . . I have my face tattooed and my ears pierced—what would the Spaniards say should they see me in this guise?"

The subdued Indians gave Cortes many gifts of tribute. Among them were their choicest maidens. And one of these was the slave girl Malinal.

7. CONQUEST OF MEXICO

Malinal had grown up to be not only pretty but bright as well. She spoke Nahuatl as her native tongue, but she had also learned a border Maya dialect known as Chontal, as well as Maya proper. She could talk to Aguilar and Aguilar could then translate into Spanish for Cortes. Malinal proved herself such a brilliant and valuable helpmate that some scholars are tempted to say she was the real conqueror of Mexico.

It was in 1519 that the Indians gave her to the strangers, and this was on the far frontier of the Aztec empire. That empire was a land larger than all Spain, filled with towns and cities. It had a population of eleven million or so, nearly three times that of Spain. And these were not Indians like the peaceful Arawaks and the disorganized Caribs. They were disciplined fighting men. City after city could send out, almost at a moment's notice, armies of thousands of soldiers who loved war. To get to the Aztec capital the Spaniards would have to pass through much of this territory. But Cortes was determined to go. For even on the far frontier coast the great city of Tenochtitlan, sometimes called Mexico after the Aztecs' other name, was famous. It was the center of the world. And the all-powerful Montezuma who ruled there was obeyed to the ends of the earth. What wealth of gold might not be found there!

The Spanish expedition consisted of only some 400 men. But by the end of the year they held Montezuma prisoner in the center of the city of Mexico and through him commanded all the country.

How did they do it?

They had better weapons—but not that much better. The quilted armor of the Mexicans was actually superior to Spanish steel breastplates. And the sight of horses and sound of cannon didn't win any more quick victories for the Spaniards. The important thing was Malinal. Because of her they had to fight only once before they had won powerful allies. For Malinal's keen eyes and ears noted everything. Time and again she learned of secret plans against the Spaniards and gave them warning. The little army of 400 would have been wiped out a dozen times over had it not been for her devotion to Cortes.

Montezuma got word of the coming of the bearded men almost at once and was deeply disturbed. He knew how few the Spaniards were, and yet—— Had not Quetzalcoatl, the bearded white god, born in the year of Ce Acatl, said that in another year of Ce Acatl he would return from the sunrise to reclaim his kingdom? And this year was another year of Ce Acatl!

The king sent gifts to Cortes—a solid gold disk big as a carriage wheel, carved to represent the sun; a larger silver disk, carved to represent the moon; a helmet full of grains of gold; 100 bearers loaded with other gifts of richly embroidered mantles, gold ornaments, crests of feathers. Montezuma expressed his friendship. But he politely refused to let the mysterious strangers visit the city of Mexico.

The stupendous gifts only whetted the Spaniards' appetite for more. Cortes sent back messages of friendship. At the same time Malinal worked hard to win allies. And the expedition kept right on towards Tenochtitlan.

All the wonders the Spaniards had seen on the way had not prepared them for the cities around Lake Texcoco—the towers and temples rising out of the waters; the long straight causeways jammed with curious crowds; the officials with dazzling plumes hung with jewels of gold and jade and pearls. Then came the capital, the city of Mexico. The soldiers asked each other if they were dreaming. "For it is," wrote Cortes, "the most beautiful city in the world."

The Indians were just as excited about the strangers. They took in with astonished eyes their strange weapons and dress, the one Negro among them, the 14 or 15 horses and one colt, the two greyhounds, and the loads of mysterious baggage on the backs of Indian servants.

Montezuma himself was brought out in his litter to meet them. His priests fumigated Cortes with incense and presented him. And Montezuma quartered the strangers in the great palace of his father.

A week passed during which Montezuma showed them the city, its temples and huge market place. Then one day Cortes came calling with a handful of men and Malinal and made a prisoner of Montezuma. It took Malinal two hours to convince the emperor it would be best for him to come along quietly. He went with the Spaniards to

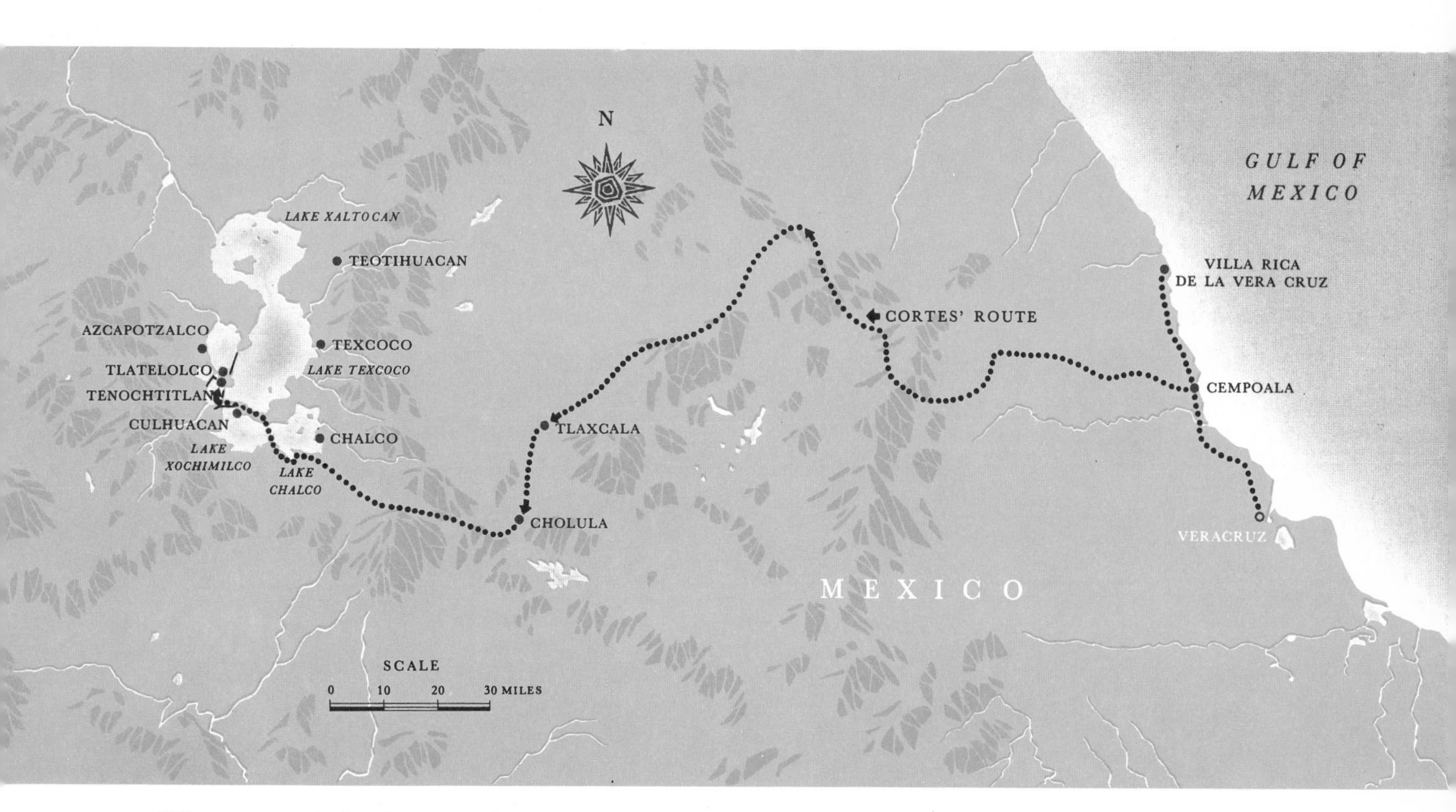

The center of the Aztec world in the 15th century was around Lake Texcoco. Dotted line shows Cortes' route to Tenochtitlan. The Tlaxcalans became allies of the Spaniards.

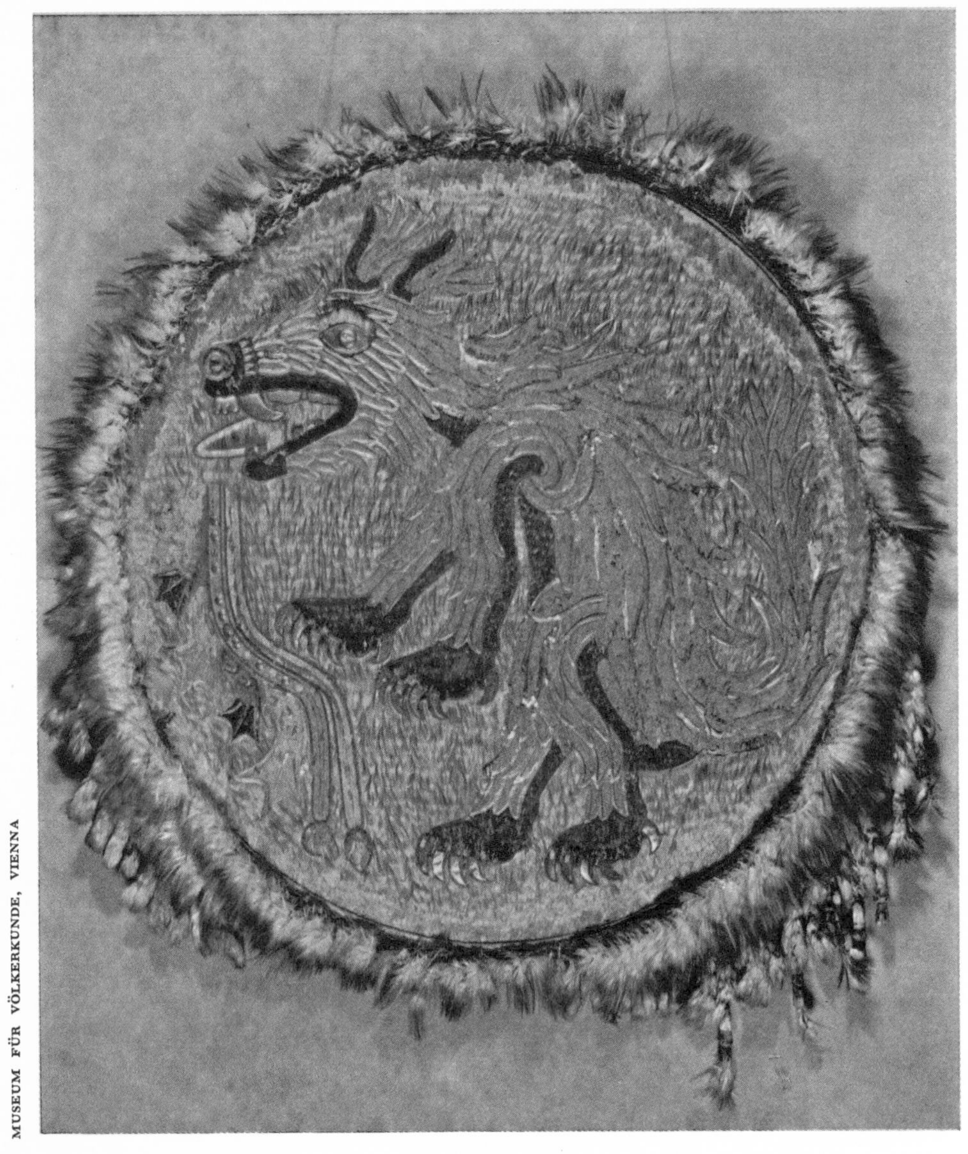

MUSEUM FÜR VÖLKERKUNDE, VIENNA

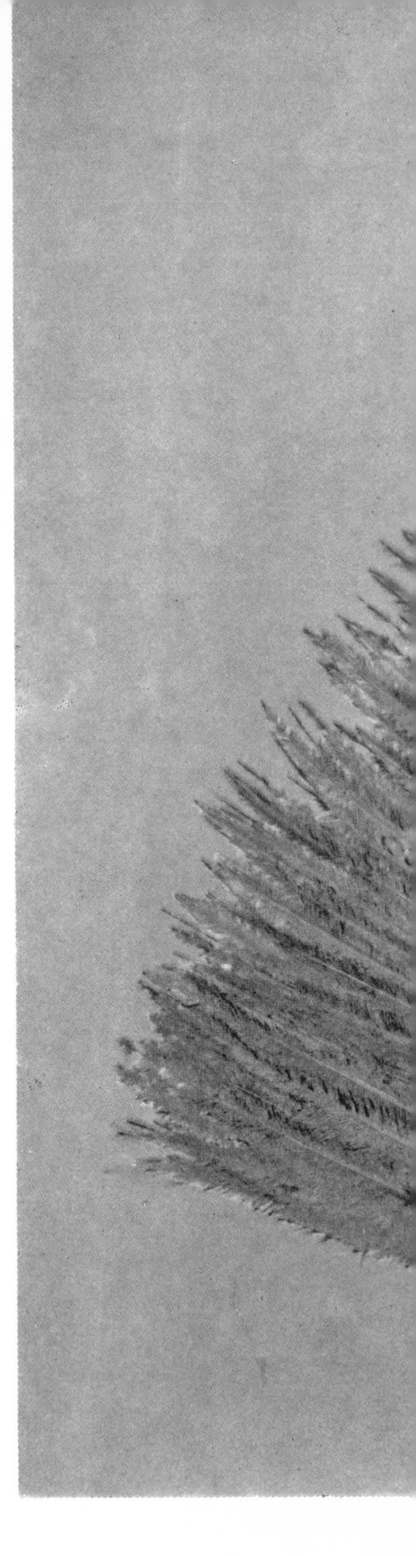

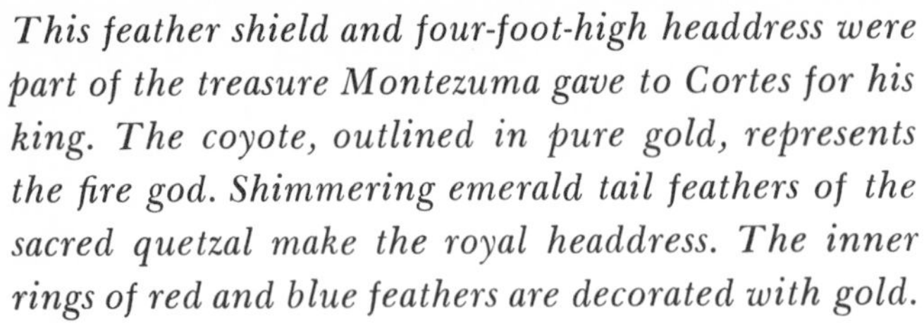

This feather shield and four-foot-high headdress were part of the treasure Montezuma gave to Cortes for his king. The coyote, outlined in pure gold, represents the fire god. Shimmering emerald tail feathers of the sacred quetzal make the royal headdress. The inner rings of red and blue feathers are decorated with gold.

their quarters.

There he swore loyalty to the strangers' king, and, at Cortes' suggestion, got together a present for the lord across the sea. It was his family's heirlooms and all he could raise from his empire. It was gold such as no monarch in Europe possessed. In nineteenth century dollars it amounted to some six million.

The Spaniards set aside one-fifth for the king. The rest they divided, with many rows, among the company. The Spanish

MUSEUM FÜR VÖLKERKUNDE, VIENNA

captains had their shares made into heavy chains of gold and wore them over their doublets.

The war was still to come, but the conquest was really over. Four hundred Spaniards had coolly taken over the capital, and that capital could—and did—raise an army of many thousands. Montezuma had but to lift a finger and the little band of strangers would be stormed under and destroyed.

He didn't lift it—perhaps because of the smooth speeches of Malinal. Or maybe

Montezuma really believed the strangers were gods—would anybody but gods have so much audacity? He was anxious to get the strangers to go away. But he was anxious not to anger them.

And so months passed. In the spring of 1520 a new army landed at Veracruz—1,400 men under a red-bearded arrogant soldier named Narvaez. He had authority to capture Cortes dead or alive.

Cortes took 250 or so of his men and 2,000 of his Indian allies and as much gold as could be carried and went to deal with him. He left Pedro de Alvarado—blond, handsome, and vicious—in charge. It was a mistake. The priests were beginning to urge death for the strangers. Rumors of this reached Alvarado, who rashly ordered an attack on the people dancing at the feast of Huitzilopochtli.

By the time Cortes had got rid of his enemy and come back to Tenochtitlan with a thousand of Narvaez' men, he found war in the city. He sent word to Montezuma. Let him go out on the terrace and try to calm his subjects. Let them stop the attack and the Spaniards would go away.

Montezuma had had more than enough. "What does he want of me now?" he burst out. "I neither desire to hear him nor to live any longer, since my unhappy fate has reduced me to this situation on his account." But he did go. According to one account, he stood at the railing of a terraced roof and addressed the people below him. Three stones and an arrow struck him. In a little while he was dead.

The Spaniards had to fight their way out of the city. Cortes and Malinal escaped, but more than 800 Spaniards were killed in the fighting. Many were drowned in the canals by the weight of the gold they were trying to carry off. Many were captured and sacrificed. The gods ate well on this midsummer Night of Sorrow.

A year later Cortes was back with armies of Indian allies to attack Tenochtitlan again. Cities which remained loyal to the Aztecs were put to fire and sword. Their populations were branded on the face and sold as slaves. Prisoners of war with whose people there was no chance of making peace were sent home with their hands cut off. And captured Spaniards were sacrificed. It was a long and bitter fight. Cortes surrounded the city and held it under siege until fresh water and food became more precious than jade. The Aztecs fought like demons, from house to house, from temple to temple, and along the canals. They wanted to die fighting—and they did, almost to a man.

The battle lasted 85 days. It ended when the last few defenders in the northeast corner of the city were cut down.

About the same time white men first saw Peru.

In the early 1520s barbarians crossed the Andes from the east to plunder the Incas. They were Guaranis, bowmen and cannibals from the Chaco. In their company were a few white men, shipwreck survivors from a Spanish exploring fleet. They had been wandering around South America for five or ten years.

The Incas were used to having the Guaranis appear on their borders. But this invasion was important because right after it came a sudden pestilence—the Guaranis and their guests may have been carrying it wherever they went. And that pestilence killed the Inca Huayna Capac. He died so suddenly that he didn't have time to announce who should rule after him. He meant to have his son Huascar succeed him, and, indeed, Huascar was duly crowned at Cuzco by the high priest. But Huayna Capac happened to die at Quito in the north, where he had a separate wife and a son, Atahualpa. Atahualpa decided to be king. He made himself ruler of Quito and governor of the northern provinces and took over command of the army his father had with him when he died. It was the best army in the empire.

Five years of war followed. Atahualpa's generals won a solid string of victories for him, and the war ended with a triumph north of Cuzco. Huascar was taken prisoner.

Atahualpa himself was at the town of Cajamarca in the north when this happened, taking the natural hot sulphur baths. At the same time he got word that people with beards had arrived in ships out of the sea, with animals like llamas only bigger. There were 164 bearded ones and 62 animals.

Were the strangers returning gods? There was a legend that the god Viracocha would someday return. Had he come back to put Atahualpa on the throne? In any case what harm was there in letting the bearded ones approach?

The white men came. They were led by a hard-eyed, illiterate, 61-year-old soldier named Francisco Pizarro, a man with a lifetime of blood on his hands. Some of the Spaniards appeared before Atahualpa and invited him to pay a visit to their quarters.

The next day Atahualpa came in his litter accompanied by several thousand soldiers. Pizarro, who knew what Cortes had done in Mexico, was all set to take the Inca prisoner. There was a shout of "Santiago!" The cannon was fired and the cavalry rode down the Indians. In a matter of minutes Atahualpa, dragged from the litter, was in the Spaniards' hands.

GILCREASE INSTITUTE, TULSA, OKLAHOMA

Last of the Inca rulers. This miniature painting of Atahualpa was found in Peru during the 1830s.

There are no heroines in the story of the conquest of Peru and no heroes. It is a simple tale of double-dealing and violent crime. With the sacred Inca as a hostage, the Spaniards were safe from attack. Pizarro ordered Atahualpa to produce a ransom. Twice as much treasure was gathered as Cortes got out of Moctezuma. Gold was torn off the Temple of the Sun at Cuzco to satisfy the white men. And when all the gigantic ransom had been gathered, melted down, and distributed, Pizarro had Atahualpa publicly strangled.

Again a conquest was completed although the war was still to come. In Peru it was a savage, stubborn war. It lasted 40 years in the empire itself and 300 years longer in the border country to the south. In the wild Chaco and Montana to the east, it isn't over yet.

8. COLLISION OF TWO WORLDS

Columbus had discovered America and nothing would ever be the same again. Back in Spain the talk was all of gold, colonists, exploration, Indians. Even people who had never set foot in a ship had seen the naked savages, for in 1498, six hundred Caribs had been sent to Spain to be sold as slaves. A Council of the Indies was set up in Seville. And many laws were passed to deal with affairs across the sea. Queen Isabella meant kindly by her new subjects. One of her early laws was to prohibit the Indians from taking so many baths because it was bound to injure their health.

The king and queen meant well, but they were 3,000 miles and many months away. Things in the colonies didn't go exactly as planned. The governor handed out the conquered lands to colonists and "commended" villages of Indians to the care of *encomenderos*. The *encomenderos* had the right to force the Indians to work, but only as free men and for pay. However, it turned out in most cases that they worked as slaves and without pay. Men hanged themselves and women killed their own children rather than submit.

Bartolome de Las Casas, the first priest ordained in the New World, thundered against this evil system, but it continued. The *encomenderos* loved being feudal lords and getting their plantation work done for nothing. The Council of the Indies kept hoping things would get better. Everybody agreed that the system was certainly very bad, but, after all, it was certainly practical.

Bartolome de Las Casas was appalled at the brutality of the Spaniards. He went back and forth to Spain, pleading on behalf of the oppressed Indians. "To these quiet Lambs," he wrote, "endowed with such blessed qualities, came the Spaniards like the most cruel Tygres, Wolves, and Lions." He knew all about it, for he had seen Cuba "reduced" by blood and terror. The "reducer" was red-bearded Panfilo de Narvaez. The priest had called down a bitter curse upon him, but that had not helped the Indians. One of Columbus's gentle Tainos, being burned at the stake, refused to be baptized—he was afraid he would find more Christians in heaven.

One after another, expeditions sailed from Espanola (Santo Domingo) and then from Cuba. They hurled themselves against Panama, searching for gold and pearls and the Southern Sea. One by one the expeditions broke. Yellow fever and the poisoned arrows of the people were too much for the Spaniards. The Indians were often friendly at first, but what with slaving, murder, torture, and plunder, they soon learned better.

As we have seen in the case of Cortes, the Indians fought back hard. If not for the friendship of Malinal and the Indian allies, Cortes and his band would certainly have perished. And it was nearly always that way in the New World. The Conquistadors who won usually did so with some Indian help. The first expeditions to Panama met with disaster. Not till Balboa, discoverer of the Pacific, came was there any success. And Balboa succeeded and got to the Southern Sea because he won the love of a chieftain's daughter and made friends with a chieftain's son.

RARE BOOK DIVISION, NEW YORK PUBLIC LIBRARY

Bartolomé de Las Casas worked tirelessly to end the Spaniards' cruelty toward the Indians.

And now expeditions went forth from Panama as a base, from Mexico, and later from Peru, and from every little foothold in between. They went forth like wolves plunging into a giant carcass.

Racing each other for the fattest mouthfuls, the Spaniards went up and down the seas, the shores, the mountains, and valleys. Might there not be another Mexico, another Peru just beyond? The Indians always said so. (Why not? It was what the white men wanted to hear and the best way to make them go away.) Mines of gold or silver might be anywhere. Or spices or pearls. And there were sure to be slaves to be taken and souls to be saved for Christ.

Fabulous mines were discovered in Peru and Mexico and worked by Indians under the lash. Tombs in Colombia and Ecuador were rifled for their unbelievably old golden furnishings. One troop of Conquistadors even rode around with stirrups and scabbards of solid gold.

There was a lot of fighting. Conquistadors fought the Indians and fought each other. In the Maya country at one time five different Spanish adventurers were stalking each other and fighting the Indians at the same time. The Mayas gave up hard. Pedro de Alvarado—that same vicious Pedro whom Cortes left in charge of Montezuma while he went off to deal with Narvaez—taught the obstinate Mayas a lesson. He caught and hanged their women and children. Then the most beautiful Maya girls were picked out and either hanged or thrown to the packs of fighting dogs to be eaten alive.

Fighting, exploring, murdering, plundering, the Conquistadors made bloody contact with a big slice of the New World. By the middle 1530s they had already got a glimpse of most of the people in the Americas. For three-fourths or more of them were in the Mexican and Andean region. In all the enormous area north of Mexico, there were probably not more than between one and two million souls.

Even so the Spaniards had only scratched the surface of the Indian world. For the number of separate tribes, bands, and groups then living in the Americas was almost beyond counting. More different languages were spoken in North America than in all the Old World put together. And in South America the variety was still greater. According to the lowest guess, there were 500 to 1,000 different languages in North America and at least twice that many in South America. Most of the New World's nations had as yet received no hint of the collision with another world. In America north of Mexico very few of the villages, tribes, kingdoms, and confederacies had heard of the people from heaven. And fewer still had seen any.

Time went on as it always had. And perhaps nowhere had it gone on more uninterruptedly than in certain areas of what is now the Southwest of the United States.

9. HOHOKAM, ANASAZI, PUEBLOS

The Papagos and the Pimas are close cousins, speaking dialects of the same language. The Papagos live in the deserts of southern Arizona, and the Pimas live in the near-dry river valleys. Both are descendants of an earlier people who had lived in the same country in just about the same way for more than 9,000 years. They have been given the name Hohokam. It is a Pima word meaning "Those Who Have Gone."

While the Mayas built their city centers and abandoned them, while the Toltecs came and went and the Aztecs rose to power, these people lived quietly in Arizona. They planted their corn, beans, cotton, and pumpkins, hunted the little desert deer, and squeezed some sort of use out of nearly every wild plant that grew on their sun-dazzled ground.

They had many things familiar to the whole belt of farming villages that ran all the way south to the Valley of Mexico and on to Central America. They had the same little clay figurines, the same snake and bird designs, the same ball courts and rubber balls to go with them, and the jingling copper dance bells that were traded from Central America and Mexico. Around A.D. 1000, someone among the Hohokam stumbled on the idea of etching. Maybe it was done by using a weak acid of fermented cactus fruit juice. Maybe it was just one family's magic secret. In any case, after a century or two, the Hohokam stopped decorating sea shells with etched designs. It is the first known use of etching in the world.

Stone houses of the Pueblo Classic Age nestle in a cliff at Betatakin in northern Arizona.

The Hohokam center was in the region where the Gila River meets the Salt, the neighborhood where Phoenix stands today. The people built miles of irrigation canals. We don't know how many thousand acres they watered, but the canals were a tremendous undertaking that called for as much work as the city centers built in the Valley of Mexico. Single ditches that ran for 16 miles have been surveyed. Some were 25 feet wide and 15 feet deep. One network along the Salt River totaled 150 miles.

Irrigation was something the Hohokam had in common with the mighty civilizations of far-off Mexico. But some things they had not at all in common. The Hohokam were absolutely democratic. And they were resolutely peaceful.

They had no classes. Everybody lived the same way. Each family had the same sort of earth-and-pole house built over a dug-down living-room floor. And even the house of the most holy priest was only somewhat larger than the others, if different at all.

They didn't like war. When later on war was forced on the Papagos and Pimas, they fought well and hard. But they felt that war was something unclean. When a successful warrior returned bringing the four hairs of his enemy's head that served him for a scalp, he had to undergo the 16-day cure for insanity. Many Indian peoples required cleansing ceremonies for warriors who had killed. But seldom did they have to call for quite so much cleansing. The war speeches of the Pimas have been collected. They all end with the same words: "You may think this over, my relatives. The taking of life brings serious thoughts of the waste. The celebration of victory may become unpleasantly riotous."

Northeast of the Hohokam country was the land of another peaceful people known to us as the Anasazi. This is what the Navahos called them when speaking of the ruins of their long-ago towns—Anasazi, "Ancient Ones." Their early center was where the four corners of New Mexico, Colorado, Utah, and Arizona meet. It is a country of red-rock canyons and sagebrush flats, of grasslands in the foothills, and juniper and pine in the mountains.

The earliest Anasazi were called the Basketmakers because when in 1893 some ranch boys found the first skeletons in a shallow cave in Grand Gulch, Utah, there was a huge basket over the head of each one. No pottery was found, only baskets. Some of these were so tightly woven they would hold water. The Anasazi could cook in them by dropping hot stones into the water.

Like the Hohokam, these Ancient Ones lived in houses built over a dug-down floor. But after a while they began building their houses entirely above ground, of log and adobe and then stone. At about the same time—the 7th or 8th century A.D.—they began to make pottery. They also added cotton and beans to their crops of corn and squash. And slowly their way of life changed. A mother and her married daughters and their families would join their houses together in a single structure. And finally a whole village lived in the same many-roomed building of several stories.

Pit houses were built, too, but not to live in. They were religious centers for the men. Usually they were round, underground chambers. To get in and out the inhabitants had to go by a ladder through the roof. There were paintings of gods around the walls and a mysterious hole in the floor, the *sipapu*. The sipapu was to remind the Indians that their first ancestors came from the belly of the earth. Today these underground chapels are called *kivas,* from their Hopi name, and the descendants of the Anasazi we call the Pueblo Indians. *Pueblo* is the Spanish word for "town."

An Anasazi pueblo was a right little, tight little, closed little world. And years passed, sometimes a great many, and nothing out of the way happened. The people sang up the corn, called the rain with puffs of pipe smoke and clouds of eagle down, danced together with their mother the Earth, worked together, laughed together. Gradually they became grandparents and died and their grandchildren became grandparents—and still nothing changed, nothing interrupted, nothing interfered.

Tree rings of house timbers at a single site in the Canyon de Chelly date from A.D. 348 to A.D. 1284. For 936 years people lived on that same site. At Mesa Verde, Indians lived for 1,000 years. On the mesa top at Acoma, Indians have been living for 600 years to date. The Hopis have lived on or about their same three mesas in Arizona for 1,500 years, and their present-day village of Old Oraibi has been occupied steadily for some 800 years.

But looked at over long periods of time, the Anasazi did move around. They merged and split. They built and abandoned towns. Generally they had to go for the reason that their old fields had died through drought or erosion. Sometimes disaster

SOUTHWEST MUSEUM

Basketmaker remains from about A.D. *700. The pottery takes its shape and design from the basketry it replaced. The beans, squash, and corn were grown by the settlers.*

struck suddenly and they had to flee. This happened to a pre-Pueblo people called Sinagua when a volcano erupted in 1066 and left the scar now called Sunset Crater near Flagstaff, Arizona. Years later when farmers again came to the fields which now were fertile with volcanic ash, Hohokam and Pueblos came with them.

The Pueblos had their Golden Age too. It was around A.D. 1100-1300. By that time there were Indians living the Pueblo way from Nevada to Texas. They were different tribes and spoke different tongues, but they all lived in a remarkably similar way.

What that way was, the ruins of a dozen or more giant community houses are left to show us. They are in the canyon of the Chaco River in New Mexico, and the best known of them is Pueblo Bonito. It rose to five stories once and had more than 800 rooms as well as many kivas and dance courts. Built in the open, this pueblo covered three acres of ground. It was the biggest apartment house in the world until 1882 when a bigger one was built in New York. Pueblo Bonito could have housed well over 1,000 people. It was added to and added to for 150 years, from the year 919 to 1067.

In the 1200s, the Pueblo world began to shrink. Tree rings tell us of a long and murderous drought of 23 years. The people drifted away from the great pueblos until many were left abandoned.

But the rainless years weren't the whole trouble. Very likely the Apaches and Navahos began to push their way in from the north about that time. They had new-style bows and knew well how to use them. The Pueblos moved away. And now the center of their world shifted to the upper Rio Grande River in New Mexico.

Some called the river by one name, some by another. Among some the people were divided into two groups, the Summer People and the Winter People, and each group took turns running the town for half a year. Among others the head of a certain society became the town leader. Among most, men grew the corn and women ground it. Some wore cotton clothes and some wore buckskin.

But for all of them the Milky Way was the Backbone of the World. And all knew the powerful gods, the kachinas, who had granted men the right to wear masks and represent them in dances of prayer.

All knew that the world's balance was a delicate thing and that you could upset it by wickedness, ignorance, or accident. Evil magicians did it on purpose. There were beasts, trees, snakes, birds, mountains, stars, all of which had supernatural power. There was a right way of living with them. You had to present a newborn baby to the sun, for instance. You had to perform a great many rites to make the corn grow high.

Some of these rites were very complicated and called for priests. But others did not. Everybody turned out to clean up the pueblo for the harvest so "the corn will be glad we bring it in." Anyone could pray anywhere so long as it was done with a good heart. If you were a man, you could offer

Pueblo Bonito, which covers more than 3 acres in Chaco Canyon, New Mexico, was the world's largest "apartment house" until 1882. It could house more than 1,000 people.

NATIONAL PARK SERVICE

a feathered prayer stick. If you were a woman, you could offer a sprinkle of cornmeal.

The first rule of this Pueblo living was: everything in moderation, nothing too much. In Mexico people sought to have religious visions and ate powerful drugs to get them. Not in the pueblos. At Zuni they did indeed use a narcotic, but that was to put a patient to sleep while a broken leg was set or a tumor cut out. And even then it was given only to women—men didn't need such nonsense.

Work was the rule, but the rule was also to make it fun if possible. Do it the right way. The right way was for the women to make a social bee of the never-ending work of grinding corn. The right way was to work together and have a man at the door of the grinding room play the grinding song on a flute.

Do it the right way. Live the right way. Live in moderation. Live in harmony with each other and with the past and the rest of the living world. Joy is all around you, it is as inexhaustible as air. Accept it. Accept life and joy, be happy. That was the Pueblo creed.

On a day in May in the year 1539, foreigners appeared at the crowded little pueblo of Hawikuh, the Zuni town farthest west. They were Indians from the land of the parrot traders to the south, some 300 of them. But they were led by a man who was black, something the Zunis had never seen. The Negro was Estevanico (Stevie), slave of the Spaniards. He discovered New Mexico. He was an old hand at meeting strange Indians, but whatever he did at Hawikuh was not the right thing.

The Zunis, after consulting a long time, took up their bows and killed him. Some of those who were with him fled with the news to the Franciscan friar and his company of Indians, whom they had left down the back trail. The friar sprinted back for Mexico "with his gown gathered up to his waist." But next summer a terrifying army of white men and more Indians from Mexico appeared, and hundreds of weird beasts that were horses and mules. It was the expedition of Francisco Vasquez de Coronado, who had heard rumors of seven cities of gold and had come to find them.

The Zunis from six or seven other towns collected at Hawikuh. They sent the women, children, and old people to hideouts, and telegraphed each movement of the oncoming strangers with smoke signals from town to town. When the strangers arrived at Hawikuh, the Zunis were defiant. The Spaniards begged them repeatedly to submit without fighting, but the Zunis came up to the very heels of their horses to shoot arrows at them and try to drive them away. At last the cry of "Santiago!" was raised and the Spaniards stormed the town. The taking of it was only the work of an hour.

In September the main force of Coronado's expedition came up with more horses and mules and even odder animals—pigs, sheep, goats, cattle—as well as white women and children. They moved on to the pueblos of the Rio Grande for the winter.

There were some 20,000 or 30,000 people in the pueblos. That winter they were usually working for the Spaniards, who took their food, blankets, women, and houses. And when the people resisted, the Spaniards took their lives by sword, fire, and rope. The Spaniards really liked these brave and modest little people. Coronado

These kachinas, painted by Hopi Indian artists, represent ancient religious spirits.

Masauů

Ahül

Tawa

Eototo

Kokle

Hehea

HARVEY CA

Acoma, perched on a steep-walled mesa top, seemed safe. But the Spaniards forced their way up.

honestly did try not to kill them. But why wouldn't they submit? Unfortunately the Pueblos didn't have any history of submitting. They didn't know how. Even the quiet Hopis, whose name means "Peaceful Ones," insisted on a fight.

In the summer Coronado led his army eastward, still looking for cities of gold. He came back discouraged. The next spring all the strangers trailed away, leaving only two friars as missionaries. They were killed—probably the first time they tried to stop the dances of prayer.

No white men came again for forty years, and then just a few. But in 1598 a whole population arrived—400 men, women, and children, 7,000 head of stock, and more than 80 wagons. The land of the Pueblos was being colonized.

Only the desert pueblo of Acoma, perched on its steep-walled mesa, was hard to take. The Spaniards fought their way to the top, killed the warriors, and took 500 women and children away for trial. The children under twelve were put in the care of priests. The women and older children were given 20 years of slavery. The few captured warriors, besides getting the 20 years, were sentenced to have one foot cut off. Two Hopis who happened to be visiting Acoma at the time of the attack were sent home with their right hands cut off. Let it be a warning!

The Pueblos stood the Spanish rule for 50 years. Then they joined with their ancient enemies, the Apaches, and tried to raise a fight. It was beaten down before it got started. Then came a string of disasters —famine, plague, and Apache attack—and after that, upheaval.

An Indian by the name of Pope came back from several years in prison. Pope was filled with bitterness over the punishments he had received. In the summer of 1680 he organized a real rebellion. The maddened Indians murdered priests and piled their bodies on the altars. They slew families on outlying farms. They held Santa Fe under siege for days until the Spaniards broke out and fled down the river. They wiped out nearly a fifth of the Spanish population. The rest fled.

And the celebration of victory became unpleasantly riotous. Not only churches and houses were burned. Pigs, sheep, anything living or dead that had been brought by the Spaniards was burned. Pope saw to it that the Indians at once rebuilt their kivas, made masks, and performed their dances. "God the father of the Spaniards, and Santa Maria, their mother, are dead!" the people sang. Pope ordered that nothing should ever again be used that the Spaniards had brought, not even the plants they had introduced—watermelons, chilis, onions, peaches, and wheat. But here he went too far. The people who saw God in every flower and knew plants by their first names —plants would answer you if you talked the right way to them—obeyed in everything except with regard to the seeds.

For twelve years the Indians were their own masters. Then the Spaniards came back and reconquered all but the Hopis, whom they just chanced to overlook. The fighting was heavy and brutal. And when at last the people rebuilt their towns, they locked the years of war away, and never, as a people, returned to them.

But neither did they submit. The dances and the old ways continued, secretly in the kivas if necessary.

SMITHSONIAN INSTITUTION, BUREAU OF AMERICAN ETHNOLOGY

This photograph showing medicine priests practicing a cure in a kiva was taken in 1890.

TONY LINCK

A quarter-of-a-mile-long earth mound in southern Ohio. It represents an uncoiling serpent.

10. KING OF THE WORLD

When the American colonists pushed across the Appalachians, they came upon great earth mounds.

"Who built these mounds?" they asked the Indians. The Indians didn't know—the mounds had always been there.

And so it must have seemed. For we know that the earliest of these earthworks and burial mounds were built more than 2,000 years ago. They were piled up by a farming people whose center was the Ohio Valley and who have been given the name Hopewell from their site in southern Ohio. The Golden Age of this people was between 400 B.C. and A.D. 400. They made objects of art in everything from wood and mica to copper, and they traded for raw materials such as pipestone, seashells, and metal all over eastern North America from the Rockies to the Atlantic.

Later on a new order of things came into being toward the south. It centered along the Mississippi. Here stood little stockaded villages built around ceremonial centers that featured flat-topped temple pyramids made of earth with wooden temples on top. Some of these pyramids were 70 or 80 or even 100 feet high and covered acres of ground. The pyramid building went on for centuries. And even when the first Europeans came into the Southeast, some of the temples were still being used. As in Mexico, an eternal fire was kept burning in them. But in the times we know about it was renewed at a new-fire ceremony once a year, not every 52 years as in Mexico.

The people here in the lower Mississippi area were a mixture of nations with different customs and different tongues, but all were hoe farmers and grew the same crops. Fishermen used the same tackle. Hunters roamed the same piny woods, cypress swamps, and canebrakes and killed the same bears and buffalo. All rode the winding rivers in the same kind of dugout canoe or poled the swamps with the same cane raft. All boiled corn syrup and hominy from the same recipes and gathered the same nuts and berries. The village systems were more or less alike. There would be a large town of 200 or 300 thatched houses, with generally a palisade and a moat around them for defense. The town would be a center for a number of smaller communities.

The first white men in the region found many tribes. But they found also that some fifty towns had joined in a confederacy and were the most powerful group in the Southeast. Because the first Indians of this group whom the English met were living along the Ocheese Creek, the group came to be known as the Creek confederacy. West of the Creeks were the Chickasaws. They had a river port on the Mississippi where Memphis stands today. Below the Chickasaws the most important people were the Choctaws, whose language was the language of trade. And west of the Choctaws were the Natchez. There were about 4,000 of them, and they interested the white men exceedingly. For the Natchez were really a Temple Mound state that had lived on into modern times.

The Natchez were unique in North America. They had a king who was called

For many years after the white men came, most of the Southeastern tribes kept their tribal lands, shown on this map. Later the Southeast was swept almost clean of Indians. Only a few groups managed to resist removal or extinction.

the Great Sun. This king had more power over his subjects than any king in Europe—he could command their lives, their labor, and their property.

All the relatives of the Great Sun, except his own children, were Little Suns, and it was from among them that the officials were appointed. His mother or sister was the chief woman Sun. She chose the new king when the Great Sun died. Below the Suns was a class of Nobles, and below them the Honored Men, while the lowest of all were the common people. They were treated like dirt by the rest and were called Stinkards.

Now all this wasn't too different from the way things went in the Old World. But the marriage laws were astonishing. A Sun couldn't marry a Sun. All Suns, male and female, and even the Great Sun himself, had to marry Stinkards. The children of male Nobles were simply Honored Men and Women, and they, too, had to marry Stinkards. The children of Honored Men were Stinkards. But descent being traced through the mother, the children of a female Sun were Suns, the children of a female Noble were Nobles, and the children of Honored Women were Honored People. The children of two Stinkards were, of course, absolute Stinkards.

There was a constant moving of classes from the top down and from the bottom up, but not always a comfortable moving. A Stinkard who married a female Sun had a rough time of it. He had to stand in her presence like a servant. He had to praise her every remark. He wasn't allowed to eat with her. And if he displeased her, she could have his head cut off in a minute. Or have him thrown out and pick another Stinkard in his place.

The Great Sun's subjects held him in the greatest reverence. Wearing his crown of swan feathers, he was carried in a litter to the festival of the new corn. His platform bed of state was furnished with a goose-feather bolster and heaped with the richest buffalo robes and bearskins. In the mornings he was wakened by the most distinguished old men, who saluted him with respectful cries, while he didn't deign to notice them.

"These people blindly obey the least wish of their great chief," wrote a French settler in Louisiana. "If he demands the life of any one of them, he comes himself to present his head."

Now the English were in rivalry with the French for the Natchez trade; so there was an anti-French party among the Natchez. And as the French took great advantage of the Indians, it was a strong anti-French party. But the Great Sun and his brother, Tattooed Serpent, who was the war chief of the nation, were pro-French. They stood for peace at almost any price. Thus the French got away with a great deal, especially as Tattooed Serpent was greatly beloved by his people.

When in 1724 Tattooed Serpent died, the whole nation wept. His two wives, his chancellor, his doctor, his principal servant, his pipe bearer, and some other followers went to the funeral joyously, however, for they were going to the other world with him. They would be drugged and then strangled. The Great Sun grieved so wildly that he had to be restrained from committing suicide.

One warrior who had been marked for sacrifice didn't want to go. Tattooed Serpent's favorite wife sent him away. "It is not good," she said, "that you come with us and that your heart remain behind you on earth."

French friends begged this wife not to die. "Do not grieve," she answered. "We will be friends for a much longer time in the country of the spirits than in this, because one does not die there again. Men do not make war there any more, because they make only one nation. I am going and leave my children without any father or mother. When you see them, Frenchmen, remember that you have loved the father and that you ought not to repulse the children of the one who has always been the true friend of the French."

The Great Sun himself died three years later, and the new Great Sun was young. The old queen mother, Tattooed Arm, who was very pro-French, was left their sole support.

And now things got very bad. The Chickasaws, who were English allies, caused trouble by constantly trying to bring the Natchez over to the English side. And there came now as commandant of the French at Natchez a man who was a fool and tyrannized over everyone in sight. The best plantation land had all been taken up by this time. So the commandant ordered the Great Sun to move his people from the Great Village and hand over the land to him. Instantly. If not, he would haul the Great Sun down to New Orleans in irons. At the price of a lot of fowls, bear's oil, corn, and pelts, he consented to let them stay till the harvest.

The old men met in secret councils, then sent messages to the Choctaws, who agreed to join them in war and attack New Orleans. Tattooed Arm tried to warn the commandant, but he only threw her messengers in jail.

At the first frost in 1729 the Natchez attacked the French everywhere in their country, killed more than 200 of them, and made prisoners of several hundred women, children, and Negroes. Natchez warriors refused to touch the commandant with their weapons—they had a Stinkard beat him to death with a stick.

But the Choctaws betrayed the Natchez and sided with the French, so this was really the end. The French finally managed to persuade a few dozen Natchez warriors and several hundred women and children to surrender. In this group were most of the leaders of the pro-French party. The French commander picked out a few men and women for public burning. The rest, including the Great Sun and his family, were sold as slaves in Santo Domingo.

For a long while afterward bands of the Natchez ambushed French voyageurs along the river. But the largest group went into exile among the Chickasaws, Creeks, and Cherokees.

In its small way the story of the Natchez is the story of the whole Southeast, where three great Christian nations—France, Spain, and England—were on the move. All three were boldly determined to fight to the last Indian.

COLL. OF THE MINISTER DE LA FRANCE D'OUTRE-MER

A large Indian trade canoe on the lower Mississippi River. This picture is dated 1726.

11. PEOPLE OF THE NORTHEAST

Beside the lakes and rivers of the Northeast, in the occasional parklands and the long reaches of unbroken forest, lived a many-tongued people, a people differing in many ways and in many ways the same. At the time when the Old World collided with the New, they were still following the worn paths of all the peoples who had lived in the Northeast before them.

They hunted with great skill, and the Deer, Bear, Wolf, and Turtle were their brothers. They used wild plants with the magic rites of the long age before agriculture. They traded far. Volcanic glass moved from the Rockies to Ohio, tobacco from Virginia to the St. Lawrence, copper from Canada to North Carolina. Some of the bands joined in confederacies and had power over other bands.

They raided each other now and then for loot, glory, revenge, or captives. Sometimes the killing of captives had a smack of sacrifice about it. Often it was accompanied by terrible torture.

As far north as the climate allowed, corn was raised. The men cleared and burned the fields, the women planted and cared for the crops. But even where no corn was raised, these people of the forest lived in towns. Though a few of them spent much time wandering, they stopped in villages at certain seasons of the year. Some lived in single-family huts, some in long, many-family houses.

Some reckoned descent through the father, some through the mother. Some organized in clans and claimed descent from an animal—Bear or Buffalo.

Some, notably the Hurons, north and east of Lake Ontario, practiced elaborate mass-burial ceremonies. Every ten or twelve years they would collect the bones of the dead and bury them all together along with mountains of rich funeral gifts—furs and tools and arms.

The southern game of ball, with racquets, was played. French traders called it *la crosse*. Seashells strung on strings or beaded into belts were in wide use almost as money. English traders called it wampum, from the Algonquian word *wampompeag*. Nations exchanged wampum at council meetings as a pledge that they would keep their promises.

These many-tongued people of the forest enter our history to the sound of war whoops and woodland battle. But history books give us a distorted view of them. Before the white men came, there was a great deal more peace in the forest than

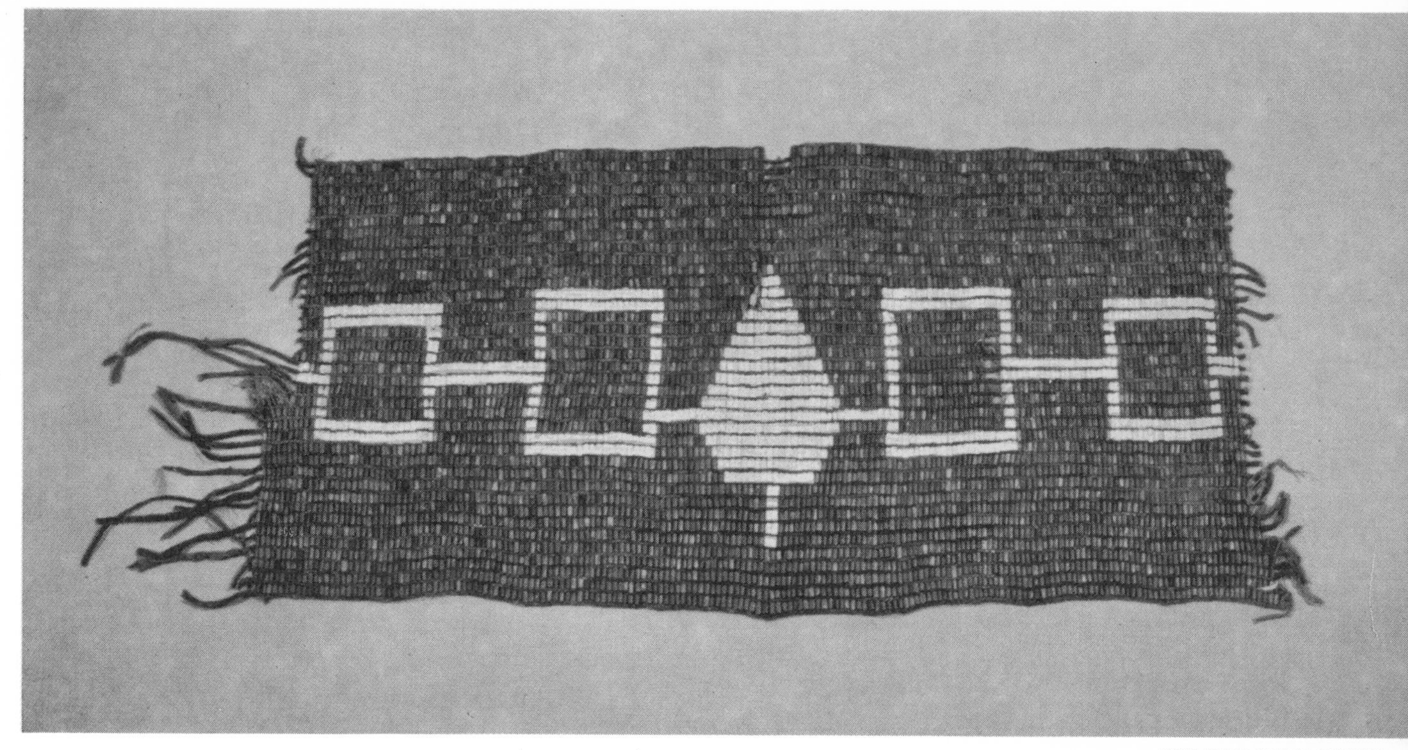

NEW YORK STATE MUSEUM

The Iroquois used wampum belts to record important historical events. The one above commemorates the unification of the Five Nations in the League.

war. In the stockaded, bark-built towns, life had its sudden storms of terror and violence, yet that wasn't the usual state of affairs. Famine was a much more common fear, uneasiness about gods and ghosts and goblins much more a part of living. There was excitement, emotion, color, and pageantry in the Indian villages. There was discomfort, but life was rich with make-believe and "style." It was made up of play taken seriously and duties carried out according to age-old rules. Above all there was in this woodland living a feeling of rightness, the kind of rightness that people feel who have lived a very long time in a very old house.

MUSEUM OF THE AMERICAN INDIAN, HEYE FOUNDATION

A Penobscot deer mask. Such masks were worn in rituals to ensure success in the hunt.

12. IN VIRGINIA AND NEW AMSTERDAM

When the English came to the New World and built their settlement at Jamestown, they found that a local Algonquian chieftain was master of tidewater Virginia. He was a great organizer. Starting from scratch, he had got some 200 villages of 30 tribes to join in a union called the Powhatan Confederacy. Powhatan means "Falls of the River," and the falls in this case were of the James River where Richmond stands today. The great chieftain, at that time some sixty years old, lived there in a village called Powhatan. So the English settlers called him King Powhatan, although his real name was Wahunsonacock.

In the first years, when the Jamestown colony was having a ghastly time and settlers were dying in batches, old Powhatan could have stamped them out with the greatest ease. For out of 900 colonists only 150 were left at the end of three years. Or he could simply have let them starve to the last man. But he did not—he sent them help instead. Captain John Smith tells us about that help and what it meant to the despairing colonists.

RARE BOOK DIVISION, NEW YORK PUBLIC LIBRARY

Powhatan as pictured in Captain John Smith's Generall Historie of Virginia.

"It pleased God (in our extremity)," he wrote, "to move the Indians to bring us Corne, ere it was halfe ripe, to refresh us, when we rather expected . . . they would destroy us." Later the Indians brought them "great store both of Corne and bread ready made."

Peace continued for quite a while afterward. There were two good reasons for that. One was that the London joint-stock company which owned and operated the Virginia colony was in business to make profit. Why start trouble with Powhatan if there was more profit to be got out of recognizing him as an independent king? The directors sent King Powhatan a copper crown to wear.

The second reason for peace was that Powhatan himself wanted it—he had an eye on trade with the English.

"Why should you take by force from us," he said to Captain John Smith, "that which you can obtain by love? Why should you destroy us who have provided you with food? . . . I am not so simple as not to know that it is better to eat good meat, be well, and sleep quietly with my women and children, to laugh and be merry with the English, and being their friend, to have copper hatchets and whatever else I want. . . ."

Many times Powhatan sent the colonists gifts of corn. Later the settlers traded for it, giving an inch square of copper for a bushel—a ridiculously small price. But later, when the shoe was on the other foot and the colonists had corn while the Indians were starving, the English governor traded 400 bushels for "a mortgage on their whole countries." Clearly the Indians hadn't the glimmer of a notion how to drive a bargain. Could businessmen feel anything but contempt for a people with so little business sense?

In the years 1609 and 1610 things were very bad at the colony. Captain John Smith tells us that if not for "blessed" Pocahontas, the 17-year-old daughter of the king, the colonists would have been much worse off. For Pocahontas, or "Frisky"—her real name was Matowaka—came often to the English fort and filled their jars with corn. "She, under God, was the instrument," Captain John Smith wrote, "to preserve this colony from death, famine, and utter confusion."

One of the colonists, John Rolfe, married Pocahontas the following year and took her to England, where she was a sensation. But at 21 the "Indian princess" died, leaving a son. A whole hallful of prominent Virginians have claimed descent from this half-Indian, half-English boy.

But the true father of all Virginia was tobacco, which the Indians taught John Rolfe to plant—to their sorrow, for tobacco decided the future of Powhatan's people. The men who organized and ran the English colonies in the New World cared about just one thing—profits. Some of them recognized no other purpose. When it meant bigger profits to have peace, there was peace; when it meant bigger profits to have war, there was war. In Virginia, profits from

NATIONAL GALLERY OF ART

"Frisky" transformed into the Lady Rebecca. This portrait of Pocahontas was painted in England in 1616.

tobacco changed everything for the Indians.

The trouble started with the fact that tobacco called for more and more land. This was not only because the colonists wanted to plant more of it. Tobacco used up the soil, and so new fields had to be found every two or three years. In the early days, by dint of fearful labor, the settlers managed to clear 40 acres. But when not long afterward an Indian village was seized at the mouth of the James River and its inhabitants driven away, the settlers suddenly found themselves in possession of 2,000 to 3,000 acres. So, at least, the report said. But even if they got only a tenth as much, it was still a wonderful inheritance. It set a pattern. Why labor to clear land when you could get it all nicely cleared so easily? Such was the thinking of some of the white men.

The Indians loved their homes, but they loved their lives more. They wept, but they moved. Each time they thought that now at last the Coat-wearing People, as they commonly called the English, had all the land they could possibly want. They had no idea of the size of English appetites for land.

This moving in on the Indians, however, was not the only source of trouble. The white men had brought over domestic animals, and these—especially hogs—damaged the unfenced Indian gardens. But if you damaged the hog, the hog's owner would damage you. And if your friends damaged the hog's owner, the English would then burn an Indian town and kill a dozen people. And then another little war was afire which Powhatan had to smother.

NEW YORK PUBLIC LIBRARY

A 16th century drawing showing the Indian town of Secotan in coastal North Carolina.

The great chief died in 1618. Four years afterward the Indians exploded and took bloody revenge for all the evils they had been made to suffer. In a few hours they destroyed a number of settlements and killed 350 colonists.

The English swore to get back at them. Year after year they punished the Indians, not giving them a chance to plant and harvest their corn. Towns were burned. Men, women, and children were slain without quarter. The heaviest losses came when the leaders of the English, promising peace, persuaded the Indians to return to their villages, then trapped and massacred them.

For fourteen years the campaign continued. In the end the Powhatan league was smashed and the English made peace with the various tribes separately. Forty years after Jamestown was founded, the once mighty Powhatans were beggars.

What went for one, went for all. All the Indians along the entire coast from the Carolinas to New England suffered the same fate. Over and over again the story was repeated. When the Indians were needed, the colonists tried to win their friendship. When they were no longer needed, the white men took away their land. Nothing personal was involved, and it is a mistake to think of Indians and settlers as being divided into two absolutely opposing camps. The "old settlers" of the colonies often had closer ties among neighboring Indians than among the newest of the settlers.

Sometimes the Indians were destroyed almost at once. Sometimes a long period of peace came before they were dismissed. In the case of the Delawares, the leading people of all the eastern Algonquians, peace or near-peace lasted more than a hundred

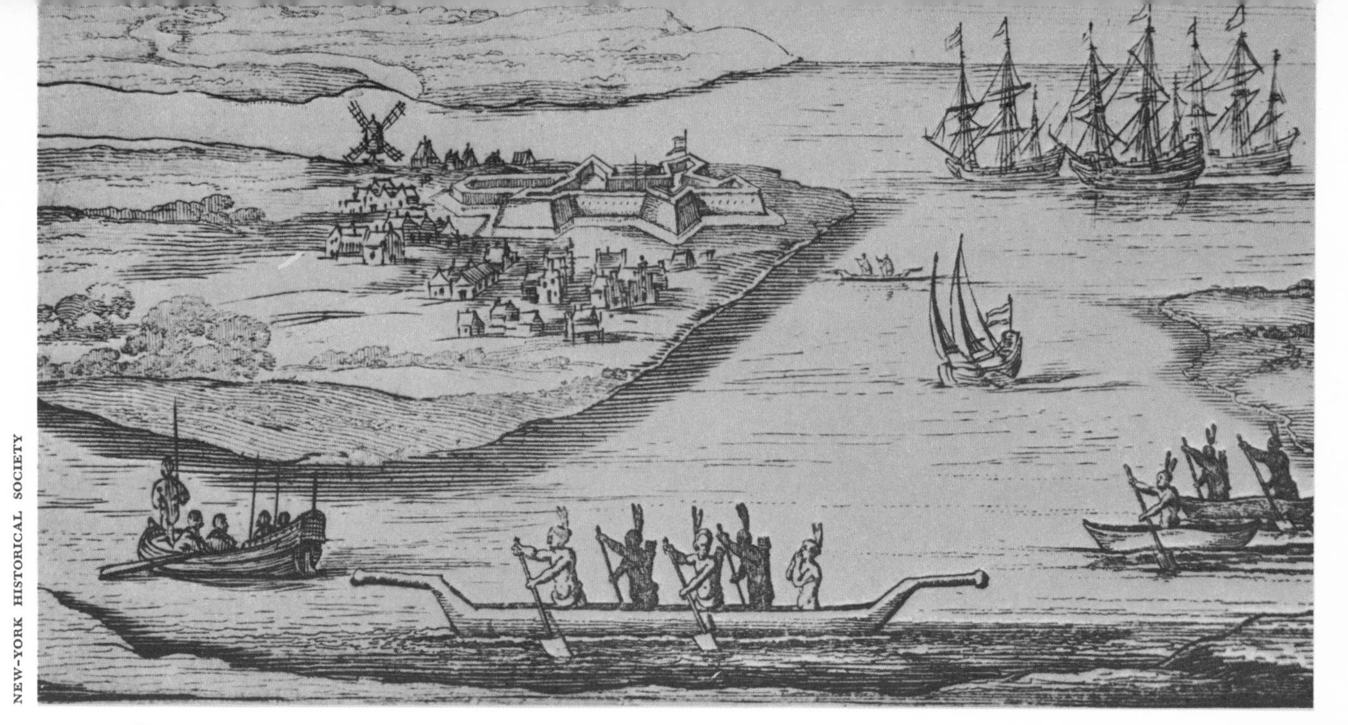

NEW-YORK HISTORICAL SOCIETY

Earliest known view of New Amsterdam. Indians bring furs while Dutch ships stand by.

years. But the end was always the same.

One of the peoples of the Delaware Confederacy lived on Staten Island and Long Island. What is now Manhattan, the Bronx, and Westchester were occupied by another Algonquian-speaking union. This was the Wappinger Confederacy. It was one of the Wappinger groups that sold to the Dutch the woodland island that is now the center of New York City.

The Dutch traded for furs with people of the inland regions, notably the Iroquois. So the coastal people who had helped the first Dutch settlers with gifts of food were now of no use to them. The Indians hung around New Amsterdam, as the colony on Manhattan Island was called, and made themselves a nuisance. They were lazy, insolent, and thievish as monkeys. Incidents occurred. When a farmer caught and killed one of their females who was stealing peaches, her relatives slew the farmer, and the tribes refused to turn these murderers over to the Dutch authorities.

In 1643, the Mohawks raided the Wappinger people. A number of them ran to the Dutch for protection, and this, the Dutch governor decided, was the moment to act. He ordered them to be massacred. The Indian refugees were lulled into a sense of security and then, while they slept in a village on the Jersey side of the Hudson, the Dutch attacked them. Eighty heads of men, women, and children were brought back to Manhattan. A Hackensack Indian was publicly tortured in a most horrible way. And the Dutch governor looked on throughout and "laughed right heartily."

In the war that followed, the Wappinger villagers were stamped out by hundreds. Even so, only 1,500 out of 5,000 were dead at the end of a year. The Dutch governor wanted to keep on fighting till the whole 5,000 were exterminated, but the company directors said "no." They were displeased by the "bloody exploit." What is more, the war was expensive. It would cost too much money to exterminate the Wappinger people. Besides, it was doubtful if it could be done. And anyway the directors could see little profit in it.

A wall built across lower Manhattan in the course of this war gave its name to Wall Street.

13. PURITANS AND "SALVAGES"

In the year 1620 a band of English colonists settled on a rocky coast west of Cape Cod. These were the Pilgrim Fathers, a grim, stern, and very industrious people.

Like the founders of Jamestown and of New Amsterdam, they were indebted to the Indians, but they had even better luck. A plague had recently swept the country of the Wampanoags to whose shores the Pilgrims had come, and the colonists found the immediate area deserted. They took over the beautifully cleared fields and felt sure that God had killed off the Indians expressly for their sake.

But this wasn't all. Behold! There appeared one day a solitary survivor of the village that had been Patuxet and was now Plymouth. He spoke to them marvelously in English. His name was Tisquantum, he said. Years ago he had been kidnapped by one Captain Hunt who had sold him as a slave in Malaga. He had escaped to England and later had been brought back home, where he had found all his relatives dead.

To the Pilgrims, Tisquantum—or Squanto as they called him—became a "spetiall instrument" sent by God. Squanto showed them how to plant corn, where to fish, and how to procure other food. He "was also their pilott to bring them to unknowne places for their profitt." Until he died in 1623, he was of enormous use to the struggling colony.

More luck was in store for the Pilgrims. A local sachem, or chief, named Samoset, who had picked up a few words of English, introduced them to the noble Massasoit, grand sachem of the Wampanoags. The noble Massasoit and his equally noble councilors remained fast friends of the English though the colonists' leaders repeatedly trampled on Wampanoag rights and liberties.

More colonists came to found settlements from Connecticut to Maine. The company that settled Massachusetts Bay sent over more than 17,000 settlers between 1629 and 1642.

The churchly colonists rejoiced over the fact that the epidemic had cleared so many heathen from the path of the Chosen People, as they regarded themselves. Especially they pointed out that God had shown his wisdom and love through a special providence that had swept "away . . . the Salvages"—chiefly young men and children.

But there were still enough "Salvages" left to be troublesome. As the settlers moved inland, the Indian nations near the coast came to be of no use whatever. In 1636, the Massachusetts Bay Puritans sent a force to smite the Pequots, the strongest Indian nation in New England. The Massachusetts Bay Puritans massacred a village and, having thus declared war, went back home.

The Pequots had attacked no English settlements. The excuse for the war was an incident dug up from four years back, an incident that was all but forgotten. It was the flimsiest of reasons. The real one was that the Pequots were powerful enough to be a threat to the colonies.

The English settlements in Connecticut and at Plymouth were dragged into the war by a hasty action. A small group of Indians, who were bitter enemies of the Pequots, came in on the English side. But the settlers' strongest allies were the Narragansets.

In June 1637 the English army and its Indian allies made a sneak attack by night on a stockaded Pequot town near the Mystic River in Connecticut. They burned the town and slaughtered its 600 inhabitants.

The only other "battle" of the war was when a crowd of Pequots was trapped in a swamp and surrendered. All the adult male captives were killed. The boys were sold to the West Indies, the women and girls parceled out among the colonists as slaves. The Pequot nation was broken.

In 1647 the noble Narraganset chief Canonicus died. The noble Massasoit died fifteen years later. And now the owners of the Plymouth Colony started a campaign—get the Wampanoags to submit and pay tribute to the colonists.

Massasoit's son Metacom, whom the English called King Philip, finally submitted, when the white men threatened war, and bound his nation to pay £100 a year tribute. This was in 1671.

It is very likely that Philip submitted only because he was playing for time. For nearly all the Indians were now coming to realize that they would be broken one by one. They were in a mood to unite. When the war did burst out, the mighty Narragansets threw in with Philip as did nearly all the lesser tribes near by. Only 500 Mohegan gunmen and bowmen came over on the English side.

It was the worst war New England has ever experienced, before or since, ancient or modern. The Indians hadn't yet learned proper tactics, but they were better armed with muskets than the colonists expected. Also, they had learned how to fix guns and had their own forges in the forests. As for Philip, he had been underrated. He showed himself now to be something of a military "genius." The Wampanoags and the Narragansets believed they could win the war, and this gave all of them remarkable courage. Fifty-two of New England's 90 towns were attacked, 12 or 13 were utterly destroyed, and 600 men were killed.

But the outcome could not really be in doubt. For by this time there were 50,000 European colonists in New England. And there weren't more than 20,000 Indians.

Philip's most famous general, a noble Narraganset sachem, was trapped by the English after six months of war and executed. Philip's wife and nine-year-old son were captured.

The Puritans were triumphant. Their famous preacher, Increase Mather, said with gusto, "It must be bitter as death for him to lose his wife and only son, for the Indians are marvelously fond and affectionate towards their children." It was more bitter than death. "My heart breaks," Philip said. "Now I am ready to die."

When the leader himself was killed, everything was over. The Puritans, as usual, hunted down survivors, and hundreds were sold as slaves. But what to do with Philip's wife and son? Some of the Puritans urged death, and quoted the Bible to back them up. But in the end King Philip's wife and the grandson of noble Massasoit were sold as slaves in the West Indies.

Here it must be pointed out again that many individual settlers and Indians were not only peaceful neighbors but close friends. It was from the various Algonquian people of New England that nearly all the common Indian words in the English language originated: squaw, papoose, moccasin, wigwam, succotash, and many more.

14. THE LEAGUE OF THE IROQUOIS

Northward from New England, northward through the unbroken Maine woods, lived other Algonquian peoples. Still others dwelt farther north, north as far as corn could grow and farther still. All the way to the freezing black spruce forests and the treeless plains around Hudson Bay there were Algonquian peoples. And all the way hunger was part of life.

All these peoples knew starving times. The less farming, the more hunger there was; for hunting is an uncertain provider even where forests teem with game. Each year had its strings of empty-handed days when hunger crept in among the lodges. Especially was this true at the end of the long winters when the woods seemed to grow magically still and all game vanished. Then the world sank into a seeming death. Then famished people ate broth made of smoke, snow, and buckskin.

The Abnaki of Maine were rather close kin, in language, with the Algonquian peoples hundreds of miles to the west, around the Great Lakes. But between the Abnaki and these language kin of theirs stretched another world. It was the world of the Iroquois. They were a great power in the Northeast.

During the first century after Columbus, five Iroquois nations, inhabiting all of central New York State, joined in a confederacy. They were the Senecas, Cayugas, Onondagas, Oneidas, and Mohawks. The white men called this union the League of the Iroquois. The Indians called it the Great Peace.

The Five Nations Iroquois were hostile toward all the peoples around them. They were even hostile to one another till the founding of their League. It was to end this state of things that, according to legend, an Iroquois statesman by the name of Deganawidah, assisted by the great and noble councilor Hiawatha, organized the League. Once there was a League, Deganawidah thought, there would be peace, justice, and a government of law. It didn't work out that way, and yet it had profound effects.

Many French writers have remarked about the exceptionally fine minds of the Hurons, an Iroquoian people who lived just north of the Five Nations. Other writers speak of the Iroquoian farms with their miles of fields of corn and beans and squash. Much is said about the well-built "long-houses" in which many families lived together, and about the log forts. Still other reports stress the dirt, the dogs, and the everlasting racket of laughter, horseplay, and constant chatter in the villages.

But when the early writers speak of the Five Nations, it is Iroquois fierceness that they stress. And most of all, the fierceness of the Mohawks. The name "Mohawk" comes from an Algonquian term meaning "man-eaters."

Far and wide the Iroquois were held to

An Iroquois warrior with tomahawk in one hand and a globe-headed club in the other.

be a cruel people. Their torture of captives was notorious. It is quite true that Iroquois women took the greatest delight in inventing tortures. While screaming women and children burned the victim with torches and gouged out bits of his flesh with jagged pieces of seashell, the captive would be encouraged to keep singing his defiant death song. This custom was true in the Southeast as well. There, too, a tortured captive was expected to keep up his death song as long as there was life in him. But it is the Iroquois who first come to mind when we think of torture and death song.

Maybe Iroquois torture was more notorious than it had a right to be, however. After all, most of their neighbors did pretty much the same sort of thing. And we have to keep in mind the fact that the Iroquois often adopted captives. Many, many times this must have happened because there were periods in Iroquois history when they may have had more adopted people among them than native born. That surely doesn't speak for exceptional cruelty.

A great deal has been said, also, about Iroquois skill in politics. But here there is good reason to believe the reports. The League of the Iroquois was one of the best organized of any of the many confederacies north of Mexico.

It was run by a council of 50, made up of the ruling councilors of each of the Five Nations. These sachems were chosen from specific families by the mothers of their clans. They were appointed for life. However, if a sachem turned out to be a bad choice, clan mothers could have him deposed and put another in his place.

There was a second class of Sachems. They were known as "the solitary pine trees." Pine Tree chiefs—who could be women as well as men—had the right to speak in council. They made up a sort of house of representatives as against the first-class sachems, who made up what we might call the senate. Anyone could get to be a Pine Tree chief, for this was not a matter of birth but of merit. For a man the usual road to Pine Tree honor, as might be expected, was by way of fame in war.

Each of the Five Nations took care of its own domestic affairs, but in international matters they were supposed to act together. In theory they did. In practice it seldom happened. Each nation went its own way again and again in making peace or war—except when it came to fighting each other. The Great Peace did keep the peace among its members.

The League was good for something else, too. It could be used to bring pressure. A Mohawk ambassador, for instance, might find it very helpful to say: "My tongue speaks for all the Iroquois." Of course, it didn't, but still . . .

The great council of the League met each summer at the principal Onondaga town and was an impressive show. Year after year, generation after generation, the sachems came together. And that was in itself bound to have an effect on the Five Nations. Even if each of them did go its own way, the magic of friendship was established. The Five Nations couldn't but feel—even if it wasn't true—that come what may, no one of them stood alone. There was a sense of unity. There was a shadowy feeling that all the way from the Seneca to the Mohawk the west wind streamed over a forest of brothers.

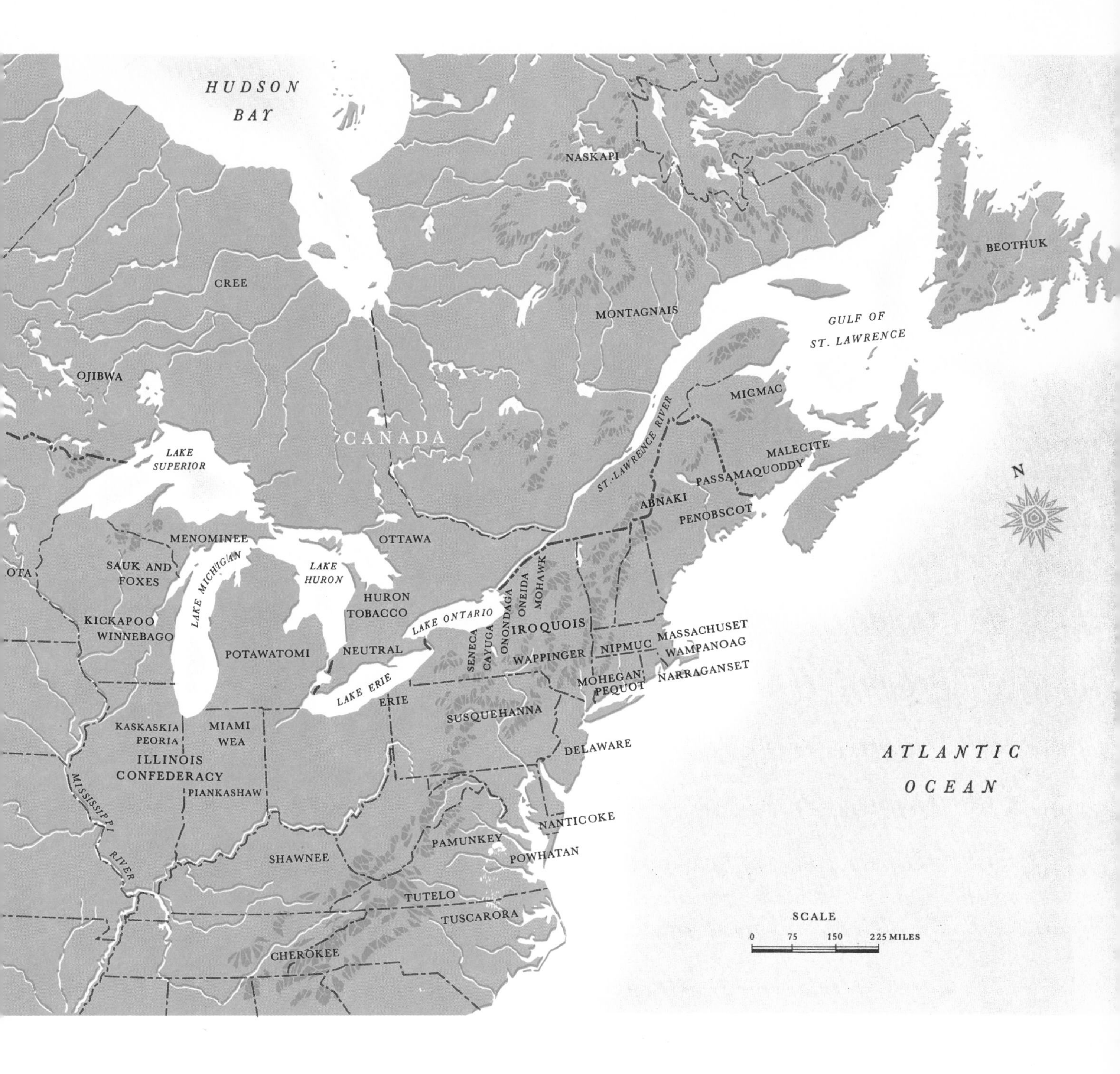

The populous Northeast, dominated by the strategically located Iroquois, was principally occupied by Algonquian peoples. As shown by the map, many tribes lived close together and maintained a delicate balance of power at the time of the white man's arrival.

15. INDIAN VERSUS INDIAN

North of Maine the first European colonists were French. The French were there—in New France, as Canada was called then—for reasons of fur, mainly beaver, and they got it by trade with Indians. So the Indians were most important to them. The French courted them and treated them like business partners.

The Indians, for their part, were happy to trade their pelts to the French. They wanted the wonderful kettles that could be hung over a fire, the metal hatchets and sharp, thin needles, the wool blankets and red cloth. But the French wanted even more the help and good will of the Indians. The Indians had woodland skills. They knew how to travel on snowshoes over winter snows. They had light, roomy birchbark canoes and paddlers to man them. Above all, the Indians knew the river-and-lake pathways to still more treasures of fur.

The Hurons and Algonquians were the first fur-trading partners of the French. The Iroquois might well have been the next, but an unfortunate affair turned them into foes.

Samuel de Champlain, the founder of Quebec, had gone on a long exploring journey with a party of Hurons and Algonquians. At the lake which now bears his name they ran into a small band of Mohawks, enemies of the Hurons and Algonquians. Single-handed, Champlain won a battle for his friends. The Mohawks, having never met firearms before, broke and ran, leaving two of their captains dead. And the Five Nations Iroquois never forgot it. From that time on — with only a few breaks of peace — they were dogged enemies of the French.

The Hurons remained partners with the French. In their white canoes they funneled through New France whole mountainloads of pelts for the French. The furs came from the enormous country north and west of the Great Lakes, where sparkling streams were thick with beaver. Trade was good. The French felt they had the Hurons, and this good fur trade, in their pocket. Their only concern was that they might lose their Indians to the Iroquois, who several times had tried to win the Hurons over. If they succeeded, it would be a calamity — then all these valuable furs would be traded to the Dutch and the English.

Now the Hurons had accepted a number of French priests as missionaries, who from the times of Champlain had acted as the governor's agents. Whenever it was called for, the missionaries stirred up anti-Iroquois feeling. As the Hurons themselves were an Iroquoian people, the priests called them the "good Iroquois." The Five Nations were the bad Iroquois.

No matter what the Hurons did, they were always "good." In the summer of 1639 they captured and burned 113 Iroquois, some of them just ordinary travelers. That made no difference — the Hurons were still the "good Iroquois." As for the Five Nations, they were those demons, those tigers, those wolves.

A terrible blow was preparing for the

To the roving hunter of the Great Lakes, home was a cluster of bark wigwams.

"good Iroquois." In 1648 Mohawk and Seneca war parties broke a truce with the Hurons that had been made in the name of the Five Nations. The Onondaga councilor who had pledged his word that no attacks would be made committed suicide in protest. But it had no effect. The following year, in the dead of winter, an army of no less than 1,000 Mohawk and Seneca warriors appeared in the heart of the Huron country. In two days of fighting they took and burned two Huron towns, then vanished with many captives and much loot.

It wasn't really a ruinous invasion. It shouldn't have been enough to break the Hurons. But it did. Panic gripped them. The people fled from their towns, and before the long winter ended, many had died from starvation and cold. Survivors kept on fleeing. They fled for years. In those two days of invasion, the mighty Hurons, who had numbered perhaps three times as many as the Five Nations, were shattered.

Some of the Huron refugees went to join their conquerors. Some emigrated to the Iroquoian nations to the west. Some scattered to the four winds.

The Huron defeat was only the first roll of thunder in the air. From now on the Iroquois frontier was alive with lightning.

At the western door of the Huron country lived a people famous for tobacco and for their vast fields of hemp, used for making fish nets. The lightning blasted the Tobacco people first. They numbered more than all the Five Nations put together. But the Iroquois broke them.

On the southwest the Five Nations attacked the people of what the French called the Neutral confederacy because they took no sides in the Iroquois-Huron quarrels. Then they struck the Erie tribe. The Erie fought back hard, and it took several years to vanquish them completely.

All this warfare was exhausting for a people that had at most numbered 12,000.

The Iroquois were sitting back, licking their victorious wounds, when the French invaded their country. They burned towns and did enough damage to destroy any nation. And the Iroquois had already been bled so white by war on top of war that in their towns there were fewer of their own people now than of immigrants they had adopted. They were forced to make peace with the hated French. Yet somehow the Great League stayed on its feet.

Then a new threat loomed from the south. The Susquehannas, fresh and feeling very tall from having conquered the Delawares, gave the Senecas and Cayugas a bad beating and then prepared to sweep the Five Nations from the face of the earth.

Only fate saved the Iroquois. A sudden epidemic broke out among the Susquehannas, killing them off in staggering numbers. Seeing how crippled they were, the Europeans along their borders fell upon them.

After that the Five Nations easily destroyed or scattered all that was left of the once powerful Susquehannas. And now, their Indian-versus-Indian wars ended (at least the big ones), the Iroquois were king of the hill.

They bounced right back from their low point. It was really astonishing how quickly they got their strength back. Their numbers swelled with immigrants. Among the Onondagas alone there were people from some 20 immigrant tribes. There was among them even a little colony of French who had chosen to become tigers and wolves.

The Great League was now *the* Indian power in colonial America, for it held the key to the entire interior of the continent. Iroquois country lay across the only good water route to the interior.

How could the French get furs from the interior with the Iroquois blocking the way?

During the 1680s and 1690s they smashed again and again at the Iroquois wall. But the Five Nations stood firm. Though the French laid waste Iroquois crops and towns, the Iroquois state remained, and it could strike back—hard.

Indeed, the Great League was now stronger than ever. It really did now begin to function the way its founders had intended. In all the 30 years of great wars the Five Nations hadn't worked together. But now they began to realize how strong their position was, and they made the most of it.

The Dutch traders were gone by this time. Only the French and the English remained. The Iroquois, though they really sympathized with the English, learned to play off one against the other and got to be artists at the game. Then they worked out a policy that would keep both the French and the English courting the League.

"We are born free," a famous Onondaga orator told a French governor, and went on to spell out what he meant. The Iroquois would go where they wished. They would allow only those to pass through their country who seemed good to them. They would buy and sell with whom they pleased.

The French raged and cursed, threatened, wheedled, and plotted by turns. They got nowhere. The Iroquois stood their ground and remained in control.

So the French changed their tactics—they couldn't let the English be the Iroquois' only friend. Thirty-six Iroquois councilors had been seized in wartime and sent to the galleys in France. The French decided it was a mistake. They got the councilors out, dusted them off, and returned them with apologies.

But neither could the English let the French be the Iroquois' only friend. "If we lose the Iroquois, we are gone," was the feeling in the Colonies. So important men traveled to Albany to meet and discuss things with the Iroquois. Four Iroquois councilors were taken to London to visit the Queen.

The Tuscaroras, an Iroquoian people who had been driven from North Carolina, joined the Five Nations in 1726. The Iroquois gave them land for a new home, made a place for them in the council, and from then on the Five Nations were the Six Nations.

In the 1700s the Six Nations had such power and glory as no other Indian nation north of Mexico ever attained. But in the northern forests there was no magnificence, no display. Dressed in blankets and dirty shirts, Iroquois sachems went off to collect tribute. The old Iroquois councilors for whom the Europeans had sincere respect had nothing glamorous about them. They wore only their dignity for show.

As for the Iroquois people in general, they had just about everything Indian hearts could desire: calico dresses and hickory shirts, log houses with fireplaces, barns filled with produce, great orchards. Sometimes they had even such luxuries as livestock and sleek, all-white canoes from the northerly Indians—their own were of elm bark and clumsy as a boot.

The Iroquois had no need to wage ceaseless war any more. Young men wanting excitement and glory still could and did go off on war parties, sometimes to very distant lands. But the old days of furiously painted soldiers and constant war were dimming into the past. Only now and then the old, old men would recite their deeds against the Erie or the French. And sometimes when they listened to the rite of the Great League's founding, they would weep. The oft-repeated words moved them: "You see the footmarks of our forefathers . . . all but perceptible is the smoke where they used to smoke the pipe together."

It was well with the Iroquois at this high tide of their nation.

BUSHNELL COLLECTION: PEABODY MUSEUM, HARVARD

These colorful Ottawa Indians from upper Michigan were fur traders of the 18th century.

LIBRARY OF CONGRESS

This Mohawk chief, the grandfather of Joseph Brant, was one of the "Four Indian Kings" who made the journey to England in 1710.

LIBRARY OF CONGRESS

16. FRONTIER PATTERN

A hurricane had swept over the nations around the Iroquois. Now the winds had died down. But the effects of the stormy years were clear to see all across the lakes and forests of the wilderness. The whole middle of the continent was strewn with wreckage. Ancient societies had toppled. Peoples were uprooted. Tribes quarreled and fought and moved around, joined and broke, joined again and broke again. And fugitives from the shattered eastern nations drifted here, drifted there. Sometimes they settled down somewhere in villages of their own. Sometimes they gathered around French trading posts on the far lakes or around French end-of-the-world trading towns in the forest, where everything was Indian except the language.

The land was filled with wanderers. They brought restlessness wherever they went. They brought strange ways and learned strange ways as they wandered. But they found new homes at last and settled among nations where they could live in brotherhood. And they tried to forget what was past.

Back in the East the hurricane didn't leave the white men's lives untouched, either. Those stormy years of Indian-versus-Indian wars had a direct effect on the English frontier. Although it is common to speak of land-hungry white settlers "clearing the Indians out," we mustn't get a picture of more and more colonists relentlessly *pushing* the frontier forward. Many forces in the Indian world helped to say where the frontier should be. Sometimes an Indian nation would encourage white people to settle on its lands so as to get their help against some other Indian nation. Sometimes wars between Indian states left the borderland shattered, and that in itself invited the white men to move in. In the early days the colonists didn't push. They didn't go looking for trouble—not till they were strong enough to handle it. Before 1800 colonists did not try to settle in large numbers on land where an unbroken nation didn't want them.

But once the white men had stepped into a territory, the story quickly changed. Then settlers kept seeping in over the border into Indian country. This was very natural. For new immigrants from Europe were often too poor to buy a place in the colony. The frontier was what might be called the low-rent district, and the fresh arrivals were willing to take their chances in it. Also, from the beginning, the frontier beckoned to outlaws, runaways, discontented people, and freethinkers.

The border jumpers brought trouble with them. What is more, the region they jumped into was often a troubled part of the Indian world to begin with. When they and their troubles had multiplied enough, a howl would go up: "Clear the Indians out!" The border jumpers weren't eager to take on the job themselves—they were yell-

For his portrait, Fox brave KishKeKosh wore a buffalo skull he took from an enemy Sioux.

ing for help. They wanted the government militia to come and do the clearing out for them.

But what the border jumpers wanted was often not what the government of the colony wanted, or what His Majesty's government across the ocean wanted. These governments often had larger aims in view. There was trade with the Indians to be considered. There was war with the distant French to be considered.

The border jumpers resented this. "Those rich, bloated, unfeeling, profiteering governors in their fine brick mansions!" they raged. "And those blood-sucking Lords of Trade in their lordly London halls!" The frontiersmen got hot when they talked about the fine gentry, sitting safe in their lace and powdered wigs. Refusing them protection against the bloody savages! Just because they didn't want to hurt their trade with the Indians! Just because they were plotting war against the French back there somewhere in the wilderness!

The settlers raised a clamor against the colonial government. They brought pressure to bear on it—and they got results. "Clear the Indians out" became government policy. It was to be the pattern of the Indian story on the white frontier.

The border jumpers sometimes got quite industrious about clearing the Indians out themselves. "I've shot and chopped and drowned the critters, I've fried 'em by the houseful and roasted 'taters in their grease," the loudmouths boasted. But they were more vicious than brave. They pitted themselves not against solid Indian nations but against tame Indians, or the remnants of broken Indian nations. In the big picture, their murderous efforts didn't amount to much.

The Indians melted away under the clear 'em out policy. Epidemics killed off a lot of those who weren't cleared out. Drink and the devil did for the rest. It made no difference who the Indians were. Descendants of foes and friends shared the same fate. By 1800 in the shabby Indian villages of Connecticut there were fewer than 100 forlorn survivors of the Pequots, the tribe that had fought against the English. There were about the same number of forlorn Mohegans, who had fought on the English side.

Some—perhaps many—escaped from the long nightmare. They went to the unbroken tribes beyond the borders. The Narragansets went to Maine and turned into Abnaki by the hundreds after King Philip's War.

But during the French and Indian wars one after another of the unbroken tribes marched to destruction in its turn.

These wars were for the most part just echoes of European wars. The French were fighting the English in Europe, so the French fought the English in America. Only here the wars were fought on the American plan, with as many Indian allies as possible.

Naturally the frontier people, being the nearest, felt the war most. Indians burned farms and villages, hatcheted settlers, carried away women and children. There was enough done to arouse fury along the frontier. But some of the frontiersmen turned this fury against their own government. They used the bloody incidents to get concessions—the scalp bounty, for instance. It was an easy way of getting damages for what the Indians had done.

The Dutch had been the first to pay money for scalps. Later on most of the colonies did the same thing. Massachusetts paid £12 per scalp in 1703, which was a lot of money, and £100 in 1722, which was a lot more. But, while expensive, it brought results. Of course no one could be sure the scalps brought in were scalps of whatever Indians happened to be enemies at the moment. Missionaries had to keep frantic guard over their Indian flocks, for it was very tempting to bring in their scalps. Some Pennsylvania settlers in 1763 collected scalps worth $1,500 simply by hatcheting three old men, two women, and a boy who were weaving baskets in a nearby town.

Many Indian nations were destroyed by the wars between the French and the English. Wherever these broken nations were near the white men's frontier, they were quickly swallowed up and digested. That is, they were exterminated. Over and over the same thing happened—and it happened faster each time.

It was thus that the country beyond the Appalachians—the Ohio country and the country northwest of the Ohio known as the Old Northwest—was taken over. The history books speak of it as "opening the land to settlement."

Perhaps the happiest to take up arms against the English in the French and Indian War were the Delawares who had moved northwest of the Ohio. They nursed a bitter grievance: the Iroquois had sold Delaware lands to Pennsylvania English, and when the outraged Delawares had protested, Pennsylvania had sided with the Iroquois. The refugees had their revenge now. After Braddock's defeat, the whole western border of Pennsylvania, Maryland, and Virginia was laid bare to them, and they skinned it alive with pleasure.

In the end, when promises were made that the land sales would be corrected, the warring Delawares changed sides. But some Indian nations on the western frontier were so wrought up against the English that they

BURTON HISTORICAL COLLECTION, DETROIT PUBLIC LIBRARY

Fort Detroit. The Indians besieged it for nearly a year during Pontiac's rebellion.

continued fighting even after the French and Indian War was over. They could not believe that the French king had really given in to the English and readily listened to French traders who assured them that he was only "sleeping."

On the western border a grand Indian alliance was formed under an Ottawa leader named Pontiac. But Pontiac's fight was hopeless because the French could not give the help that had been promised and because his alliance was not of unbroken nations but of bits and pieces of many tribes. Moreover the country which the alliance seized had already long been a center for white settlement. Yet Pontiac stood off the British for three years from the Illinois country and the Great Lakes. For six months he sustained a siege at Detroit.

Finally peace was made. It was made on the promise that the English would restrain settlement if Pontiac would demobilize and leave the restraining to them. The government genuinely tried to keep its word. But it had given a promise that could not be kept. The frontier pattern had been set. And nothing could turn back the clock.

17. END OF THE LEAGUE

The Iroquois had wisely shut their ears to the white men's appeals to come in on their side and had stayed out of the French and Indian War. This in itself helped to decide the outcome. But in the end the Iroquois did more—they actually gave help to the English.

It wasn't official—the Iroquois were all volunteers—and this is how they came to volunteer:

An English fur trader named William Johnson had settled in the Mohawk Valley and had become such a friend of the Iroquois that the English made him "Colonel of the Six Nations." He was placed in charge of all northern Indian affairs for the English crown and was given grant after grant of land till he became one of the largest landowners in colonial America. In 1755, when most of the Indian nations had gone into the war on the side of France, this Colonel Johnson walked into a council of the Six Nations. In the manner of a war chief, he threw a painted war belt among them and asked for some of their briskest men as volunteers.

Now Johnson had twice been married to Mohawk girls. The last one was Molly Brant, whose 13-year-old brother, Joseph Brant, was his special protégé. Another Indian, named Hendrick, was also related to Johnson by marriage. So when Johnson asked for brisk men, Hendrick volunteered, as did several hundred warriors. The boy Joseph went along.

In the battle of Lake George which followed, Hendrick was killed, as were many of the Iroquois warriors. But the battle was won, English America was saved, and now the war could go on to victory for the English.

The volunteers little thought that they had fought and died for the downfall of their own people. Yet it worked out that way. For once the French were beaten, the Iroquois could not play one white nation off against the other any more. Only one great power was left—England.

However, for a little while longer the Iroquois continued to have peace and prosperity. This was because Johnson, now a baronet, and his son-in-law, Colonel Guy Johnson, were their friends. Sir William put young Joseph Brant in a school for Indians which had been opened in Connecticut by a minister. Brant applied himself and came out with a good education and a hobby—translating the Bible into the Mohawk tongue.

In the late 1760s, after the French and Indian War was over and Pontiac had laid down his arms, frontier trouble again began. In this Ohio territory land had been "bought" from the Indians by speculators. The price the speculators asked of the settlers was much more than many of the immigrants could pay when a man's wages were 33 cents a day. So they jumped the border. They crossed into the territories of the broken nations on the northwest of the river. Incidents occurred, and when the Indians could stand no more, they resisted.

CHICAGO NATURAL HISTORY MUSEUM

This resolute Indian in white man's clothes is believed to be Tecumseh, America's greatest Indian leader. It was his dream to unite all the tribes into an Indian nation.

LIBRARY OF CONGRESS

Like notches on a gun handle, the 39 crosses on the tree trunk next to Hendrick stand for the number of enemies the Mohawk sachem said he had captured or killed in battle.

Then came the crack-down. The governor of Virginia made war on the Ohio bands and defeated them.

The American Revolution came soon after that. It brought many changes, and for the Great League—death. For the Revolution divided the Iroquois in war, tribe against tribe.

Young Joseph Brant had become a leading chief of the Mohawks by this time. He was in England when the war broke out and he insisted that the Iroquois should help the English. Sir William Johnson was dead, but his widow Molly, together with her brother Joseph and Colonel Guy Johnson, brought the Mohawks, Onondagas, Cayugas, and Senecas into the war on the English side. The Tuscaroras and the Oneidas sided with the colonies.

Joseph Brant led his Mohawks in border raids till "his name was terrible in every ear." The brilliant leader was called bloody, ferocious, and hateful to keep alive the strongest feelings of anger against the mother country. Many an Iroquois town was burned in reprisal. A hundred years before, the French had laid waste the Iroquois country, but now there was much more in the way of corn, barns, farms, livestock, and orchards to lay waste.

When the war was over, the Iroquois who had fought for the Tories received lands in Canada. And there, on the Grand River in Ontario, the "Monster Brant" went back from time to time to his old hobby of translating the Bible into Mohawk. Whatever the Americans thought of him, to the English he was a hero. On a second trip to England, he was a lion of society and was taken up as an intimate friend of the Prince of Wales.

In the Old Northwest, in the years between 1794 and 1811, one land-ceding treaty after another was wrung from the crushed tribes. Few Indian leaders foresaw the future. But there was one who saw it clearly and who believed that by uniting all the Indians the march of the white man might yet be stopped. This man was Tecumseh of the Shawnee nation, the greatest of all Indian leaders. Tecumseh was determined to

This portrait of Joseph Brant is believed to be a very good likeness of the brilliant Mohawk leader. Brant's proper Mohawk name was Thayendanegea.

NATIONAL GALLERY OF CANADA

hold the Ohio River as a dividing line between the races. Traveling tirelessly, he visited tribes from Wisconsin to Florida and urged them to join his movement.

When chiefs sold land to the whites, Tecumseh was enraged. He thundered against the sale of hunting grounds, preaching that land was owned in common by all the tribes and no one tribe could sell its particular tract. "Sell a country!" he argued. "Why not sell the air, the clouds, and the great sea . . . Did not the Great Spirit make them all for the use of his children?"

Though the elders often opposed him, the young warriors were fired by his vision, and Tecumseh almost succeeded in building a vast Indian confederacy. But it was too late to stop the white men's advance, for by now the frontiersman's policy of clear the Indians out had become the national policy of the United States.

It wasn't a quite open policy. There was a screen of treaties. But these treaties were wrung out of the Indians by force and were broken by the United States at will.

As the years went on, the treaties became more and more hollow forms. They were signed by "chiefs" who had no authority to sell land, in the name of nations that were little more than memories. The paper storm of these treaties moved all the way to the Mississippi. It drove the scattered survivors of the nations before it, or left them here and there as islands of paupers. Rarely did the Indians fight back. They didn't have the power to strike an effective blow; so what was the good of striking at all?

Only once was there something like resistance. Keokuk, who had gotten himself named chief of the Sauk and Fox Indians by American officials, negotiated a string of treaties giving away the Rock River country of the Sauk and Foxes. Black Hawk, the true leader of the Sauk, would not abide by the terms of these false treaties. He refused to keep his village west of the Mississippi. So the frontier militia shot up his fleeing people.

This event took place in 1832. In the history books it is called the Black Hawk War.

18. LEARNING WISDOM FROM THE ENGLISH

In the Southeast the English quickly found out who must be their friends. Here the Creek confederacy was very strong. Indeed, it held much the same position as the Iroquois League in the Northeast. It was a big power in an area of conflict between European rivals—in this case Englishmen, Spaniards, and the French.

The lands of the Creek confederacy were broad—some 84,000 square miles. And they were delightful. The English quite fell in love with the country of the Creeks, where grew every kind of wood proper for building and where the soil was excellent for corn, grapes, hemp, rice, wheat, tobacco, indigo, and fruits. There was just one trouble with this delightful land. It wasn't theirs. The "jealous natives" were in possession of it.

The Creeks, for their part, envied the English. They regarded with awe the superior wisdom of the white men. Being a highly intelligent people, they wanted, it seems, to sit at the feet of the people from heaven and learn better things. They willingly gave to James Oglethorpe, a man inspired to found Georgia as a colony for imprisoned debtors, a huge slice of land.

In 1732 a party of Creeks went to visit Oglethorpe. "We are come 25 days' journey to see you," the Micco or chief said to him. "When I heard you were come, and that you were good men, I knew you were sent by HIM who lives in heaven, to teach us *Indians* wisdom. I therefore came down that I might hear good things:—for I knew, that if I died on the way, I should die in doing good; and what was said, would be carried back to the nation, and our Children would reap the benefit of it."

Tahchee, a Cherokee, was a guide for United States troops before his tribe was removed.

On the same occasion another Indian, a very tall old man whom the English called Long King, said that though they (the Creeks) were poor and ignorant, He who had given the English breath had given them breath also. He who had made both had given more wisdom to the white men. The Indians were firmly persuaded that the Great Power which dwelt in heaven and all around and which had given breath to all men had sent the English there to instruct them, their wives, and children.

This was the reason, the Creeks said, why they gave Oglethorpe their land along the coast and the Savannah River where it "bends like a sickle before rolling to the sea."

Maybe it was true. Maybe that's how some of the Creeks really did feel. But about 25 years before this time, 1,000 of them went happily along with 50 Englishmen on a raid into Florida where Spanish priests had established Indian missions.

LIBRARY OF CONGRESS

A Seminole village in 1837. The houses were often without walls and some were raised on stilts.

They butchered 6,000 head of livestock, captured hundreds of mission Indians, and burned three priests at the stake. The Creeks sold their prisoners to the English, who needed slaves for the Carolina plantations, and everybody was happy.

It was an easy victory. For in Florida at this time the Spanish were trying an experiment. They were building a Christian Indian state. No colonies of Europeans were permitted, no conquests were to be made, and no firearms were allowed among the mission Indians. Without firearms, the Indians were sitting ducks for the English slavers, who armed and trained their Indian followers as the first lesson in white men's wisdom.

The English were especially pleased with this batch of slaves because they came from Florida. Florida was a bone in the planters' throat. According to Spanish law, any foreign slave became free as soon as he set foot in Florida. The plantation slaves knew it and headed straight south whenever they were lucky enough to get away.

Year after year the slavers returned to this happy hunting ground. By 1745 the missions lay in ruins and their thousands of converts were scattered and gone back to their wild ways. Bands of various peoples from the Lower Creek towns were moving into the country thus left vacant. And runaway slaves kept coming. The wild converts, the newly arrived Creeks, and the runaway slaves mingled over the years. In time the mixture came to be known as Seminole. Seminole comes from a Creek word meaning something like "runaways."

The English, French, and Scots who settled in the Carolinas had an unquenchable thirst for slaves. Negroes were expensive. But anyone could snare an Indian or two or three. The silly savages were so easy to beguile! Many were anxious to have their children educated by Europeans. It was a simple thing to take a child or two away and have the parents' grateful blessing into the bargain. You could sell the child or two and later on tell the parents a tragic story of sudden illness and death in spite of all you could do. Then you could shed a few tears and maybe pick up another child or two on the same visit.

Kidnapping children was simpler and quicker and got to be even more popular. The Tuscaroras of North Carolina suffered from this money-making industry for years. Finally in 1710 they sent an ambassador to Pennsylvania. Please, could they emigrate there for the safety of their children and the children yet to be born? The Pennsylvania commissioners were very sorry. But they could not let the Tuscaroras in without a written guarantee from the Carolina government that they would behave well.

The Tuscaroras made no futile attempt to get that. The next year they solved their problem by a savage attack on the North Carolina colonists. Their first act was to kill the Surveyor-General of North Carolina, who had sold a big tract of Tuscarora land without even troubling to mention it to the tribe.

As might be expected, the colonists rose up in their wrath and, with their Indian followers, quickly brought the Tuscaroras to terms. But the military expedition wasn't satisfied with the reward North Carolina gave them. So the English commander broke the truce that had just been made. He invited a large number of Tuscaroras to a friendship parley, then trapped them and sold the captives as slaves.

Naturally the Tuscaroras went back to war. It was when they were defeated again that the Iroquois offered them a new home in the Five Nations country.

Meantime the Creeks were prospering. And the English were glad of it. They needed the Creeks. The Creeks were a line of defense against the Spanish to the south, and even more so against the French who were now in Louisiana.

The Chickasaws were useful too. They were the smallest of the four "Civilized Tribes" — as the Cherokees, Chickasaws, Creeks, and Choctaws came to be called. But though they were few, the Chickasaws bordered on the Mississippi, and it was very convenient to have them attacking the French going up and down the river.

However, the Chickasaws were far from the English colonies, whereas the Creeks were next door. The English had to have the friendship of the Creeks if the southern colonies were to stay healthy and if Georgia was to survive at all. And it was easy to hold onto the Creeks, who, as has been said, were delighted to give their friendship to the English along with a goodly hunk of land. A dozen of their important men even went to England in 1734 with General Oglethorpe to advertise the new colony. They were a huge success.

Dressed in scarlet and gold and furs,

RARE BOOK DIVISION, NEW YORK PUBLIC LIBRARY

A Chickasaw. The Chickasaws were the smallest of the five Civilized Tribes.

wearing moccasins, and with feathers in their hair, they went to court in royal six-horse coaches to meet the king and queen. It was all very solemn and dignified. Only once did they come down to earth. That was when old Tomochichi, who was said to be over 90, asked for some fair trade practices. The Indians wanted standard weights and measures and reasonable prices for their goods. And they didn't want rum to be brought in.

Unfortunately the things Tomochichi asked for could not be guaranteed. The only workable trade rules were those which the Indian towns themselves could enforce. They concentrated on keeping out rum, the ill effects of which they could clearly see. For the rest, the white men were too sharp in their dealings — the inexperienced Indians couldn't keep up with their tricks. They were taken advantage of on all sides and learned wisdom the hard way. But with all that, the nations of the Southeast prospered in the 1700s, acquired livestock, and improved their methods of farming. Many took to wearing European clothes and living in European-style houses. The Chickasaws developed the famous Chickasaw horse. The Choctaws developed the Choctaw pony. But the old ceremonies stayed. There was still the green corn festival. People still played chunkey and ball. Men were still called to battle by setting up a red-painted war post. And if the battles were fought more and more for the English, why not? The English were clearly on hand

SMITHSONIAN INSTIT

George Catlin painted this picture of Choctaws playing their traditional ball game in Oklahoma. The Choctaws were the first of the Civilized Tribes to be removed.

to stay. They were an important part of the future, and that future looked good.

In those prosperous years a great many Europeans married into the Indian nations of the Southeast. If a trader was reasonably fair, he won the absolute trust of the Indians and got a chance to marry into a leading family. This meant political power as well as wealth. The half-English princes who were the children of these marriages lived by Indian customs, but their ambitions were often European. Many became personally wealthy. They had livestock, slaves, and goods. Some became petty tyrants who turned Indian law to their own purposes. Some became statesmen in their tribe and were of the greatest value to their nations, and of note in American history.

The Europeans were always pleased to see individual Indians standing out above the rest, for the white men needed some one responsible official to deal with, especially when they wanted to buy land or make a treaty. If the Indians didn't have a real chief, the white men invented one. Sometimes such a "treaty chief" was accepted by the other Indians and really became their chief. More often, he was not accepted and it led to trouble.

After the American Revolution, the Civilized Tribes turned still more to the ways, fashions, and ideas of their white neighbors. Among those who didn't change to European clothes, quite a few took to wearing a long shirt like a flowing tunic. With the customary headband or turban, this costume was curiously like that worn in ancient Mexico. Cherokee women, however, almost all dressed in European style, making gowns themselves out of cotton which they raised on their own plantations.

The Cherokees built roads, schools, and churches. They began compiling a written

LIBRARY OF CONGRESS

Sequoya, a Cherokee, devoted 12 years to inventing a system of writing in Cherokee.

code of laws in English. They adopted a system of government on the model of the United States. And a Cherokee warrior who had been crippled in a hunting accident invented a system of writing in the Cherokee language.

The name of this remarkable person was Sequoya. He had no education and could neither speak nor write English. But after 12 years of work, he invented a Cherokee alphabet. The Cherokees were entranced with the idea of a written language of their own and studied it with such enthusiasm that in a few months thousands could read and write. Then the Indians got hold of a press. And in 1828 the Cherokees began to publish a weekly newspaper.

The nation had pulled itself up by the bootstraps. But not all the tribe responded to the new ideas. Some of the Cherokees clung desperately to the ways of their ancestors. By the time the Cherokees had started their newspaper, about a quarter of the nation — some 6,000 persons — had broken away. They trekked westward to seek a new home beyond the Mississippi.

19. TIME TO TAKE OVER THOSE LOVELY LANDS

In every war between the white men, the Creeks, the Cherokees, the Choctaws, and the Chickasaws were wooed. Bribes were given. Payoffs to chiefs were made. They caused a lot of wrangling and division among the Indians. When the War of 1812 broke out, the Creek towns were sharply divided into pro-American and anti-American parties. *Red Sticks* was the name given to Creeks who took the warpath against the United States. This was on account of the Creek custom of setting up a red-painted pole in the center of a village to mark a declaration of war.

A party of Red Sticks descended on American Fort Mims and massacred most of the 350 or so people there.

A pro-American party under William MacIntosh massacred 200 of the Red Sticks. MacIntosh was the son of a Scottish trader and a Creek mother. He was an ambitious and unscrupulous man who had climbed to be head chief of the Lower Creeks.

The surrounding states organized a militia to go after the Red Sticks. Five separate volunteer generals took the field. One of them was a backwoods politician from Tennessee by the name of Andrew Jackson. The governor of his state had "bawled for permission to exterminate the Creeks." Andrew Jackson was a true frontiersman. He went right along with the policy of clear 'em out. In the Battle of Horseshoe Bend, Alabama, he managed to exterminate a pretty fair passel of them. This was during the War of 1812 in what was called the Creek War.

The anti-American Creeks, the Red Sticks, also had a man of mixed blood for their leader. His name was Menewa. Menewa and MacIntosh were deadly enemies, and the Creek War was in part a personal struggle between them.

Now the Battle of Horseshoe Bend, which started Jackson off on the career that brought him to the White House, was fought like this:

Menewa had dug in some 9,000 Red Stick warriors on a tongue of land all but surrounded by the Tallapoosa River. At the narrow neck, he had set up a breastwork of logs. A number of women and children were in a village at the river's edge.

General Jackson had on his side—besides his Tennessee militiamen—several hundred Creeks under MacIntosh and a Yuchi chief and also some 600 Cherokees. Before the battle started, Indian guides placed Jackson's 2,000 men so as to surround the Red Stick position on both sides of the river. Two cannon were set up to bombard the breastwork. After a two-hour barrage, the Indians attacked repeatedly from across the river. The village went up in smoke.

When it was clear that the Indians would not be able to overcome the Red Sticks

ALABAMA DEPARTMENT OF ARCHIVES

MacIntosh, a half-breed chief of the Creeks.

SMITHSONIAN INSTITUTION, BUREAU OF AMERICAN ETHNOLOGY

Chief Menewa, a famous Creek leader.

alone, the militia stormed the breastwork. Those Red Sticks who hadn't keen killed were driven to a thicket in the center of the peninsula, and cannon were brought up to finish them off. Then the battered thicket was set on fire and the few survivors were shot down as the flames drove them out.

Of the 900 Red Sticks only 70 were left alive, and of these only one was without a wound. Three hundred women and children were taken captive.

Menewa had fallen, hit several times by rifle fire. Sometime after the battle was over, he came to, shot a soldier passing near by, and was in return shot in the head, the bullet going in one side of his face and coming out of the other. He came to again in the night. He crawled to the river, found a canoe, and floated downstream to a swamp where some other Red Stick wives and children had remained hidden. By the time his wounds were healed, the Creek War was long ended. The Red Sticks' land had been opened up to white settlement. And all Menewa's personal property—his store, his 1,000 head of cattle and hundreds of horses and hogs—had vanished. William MacIntosh had won the contest between them for the time being. But Menewa was still alive and still very rugged. As far as he was concerned, the story wasn't over yet.

The Battle of Horseshoe Bend polished off the Creek War. After that so many Red Sticks escaped to Florida that the Seminole population was more than doubled. General Jackson found a pretext to invade Spanish Florida—he was chasing runaway slaves, he said, who had joined the Seminoles—and that started the First Seminole War. It all ended two years later with Spain giving up Florida to the United States.

This was the end of Spain in the Southeast, the end of all foreign menace in the Southeast. And the Indian nations weren't needed any more. It was time to get rid of them and take over those lovely lands.

Andrew Jackson was President by this time. One of the first things his administration did was to pass the Indian Removal bill. The Removal bill did not say the Indians should be moved by force. No, "they shall be free to go or stay, as they please," the bill said. It merely gave the President the right to offer nations other lands in exchange for Indian lands within the states or territories.

However, force was necessary, since the Choctaws, Chickasaws, Cherokees, and Creeks didn't want to move.

Alabama (which had been carved mainly out of Creek and Cherokee country) and Mississippi (which had been mainly Choctaw and Chickasaw country) and Georgia (much of which the Creeks had given to General Oglethorpe) passed laws outlawing tribal governments. It meant that Indians could not govern themselves any more and that their laws were no laws. But this was contrary to what the United States had promised them in its treaties. The Indians appealed to the federal government. They got their answer. President Jackson and his Secretary of War told them the federal government was simply unable to keep its treaty pledges.

A vast change came over the Indian country then. The Indians had done pretty well at keeping out rum. Now that they weren't masters in their own land any more and their laws didn't count, their country was overrun with liquor dealers. The Indians appealed to the President to protect them because there was a federal law about selling liquor. And again they got the same answer. The federal government simply couldn't enforce the federal law. So bootleggers crowded into the Indian country. Liquor was sold freely, and a large number of Indian citizens drank themselves into a stupor that ended only with their death or removal.

Now that the Indians were under the state laws, claims could be made against them in the state courts. But at the same time laws were passed saying that a court could not accept the testimony of an Indian against a white man. This meant that no matter how false a claim was, a white man could always get away with it. An Indian's word was no good against a white man's—an Indian couldn't legally protest.

As the tribal leaders began to accept treaties that provided for an exchange of land, white squatters and land speculators moved in by swarms. They stripped the Indians of their lands and goods by fraud, by liquor, or by force. Large numbers of Indians, many of whom had been comfortable and prosperous, were obliged to take to the woods or swamps for fear of their lives.

Crimes of violence against Indians went unpunished and almost unnoticed. Only once in a while did something get into the papers — when the person involved was prominent. An editor got indignant when a man by the name of Jones casually murdered a famous Chickasaw warrior and councilor, Emubby, who had served with General Jackson in many campaigns. Emubby was murdered without any provocation, the editor said. "When Jones presented his rifle at him, he leaped from his horse, opened his breast, and said, 'Shoot! Emubby is not afraid to die.' The wretch did shoot and the Indian fell. . . ."

Appeal after appeal went to the President and his Secretary of War. The appeals always brought the same reply: the federal government could do nothing about the abuses though it had bound itself in treaties to do so. It was not a matter of right, President Jackson said, but of remedy. The remedy was clear. Let the Indian nations be removed to the West, where they would be given land grants that would endure "as long as the grass grows or water runs."

What could the nations do?

20. THE TRAIL OF TEARS

The "trail of tears." Thousands died on the westward way.

In November 1831 the first official Choctaw emigrants, 4,000 people, started for the new lands they had selected in what was then the western part of Arkansas territory. Other parties followed the same winter.

It happened to be an unusually hard winter. The Mississippi was so choked with ice that it couldn't be crossed for days. In the Great Arkansas Swamp through which the emigrants had to struggle there was zero weather and heavy snow. And many of the Indians had left barefoot and nearly naked.

So the removal began. It went on for years. And time was to prove that the experiences of this first winter were the easiest of all—except for the Chickasaw migration.

Cholera, a dread disease that was often fatal, appeared in the summer of 1831. It centered around Vicksburg. Each summer for five years it came back. It set up a belt of death that halted most traffic. But the Indians had to go through it—the government would put up with no delay.

The exiles marched on with many a backward look and thought, for they had left their hearts behind. In spite of all the pressures on them, they wept to leave their homeland. They had lived in this sweet and luxuriant land so long! They were the descendants of the temple-mound people who had built in this region long before, and perhaps of the burial mound people who had lived there even earlier. They didn't share the white frontiersman's passion to be always moving on. This was their land, the earth to which they belonged, and they didn't want to go anywhere else. Departing Indians went about touching leaves, trees, rocks, and streams in sad farewell.

It was a pitiful medley that went forth. The educated and the ignorant, the good and the bad, those used to high-style gracious living and those from huts in the wildest depths of the forest were herded together. Weren't all of them just Indians? They were driven away like cattle, like wild animals, so they said. "We were drove off like wolves . . . and our people's feet were bleeding with long marches. . . . We are men . . . we have women and children, and why should we come like wild horses?" Many fell by the way, the aged and children first, always, from death on the march.

In 1821 and 1823, some years before the push to remove the nations began, William MacIntosh of the Creeks had made treaties with citizens of Georgia. He had ceded them 15,000,000 acres of Creek land. He had been supported in this land deal by 12 other Creek chiefs, who were under his control. But 36 chiefs, representing nine-tenths of the Creeks, opposed him. Nevertheless, in 1825, when the payoff was increased, MacIntosh and his followers signed a second treaty, giving the rest of Creek land—10,000,000 acres—to Georgia. These treaties were not only contrary to Creek law. They also went against a specific law providing the death penalty for any Creek who sold land without the consent of the entire nation in council. This sentence was now passed on MacIntosh. On May Day morning 1825, a party of Creek soldiers went to his house and shot him dead. The man appointed to execute him was Menewa, the ex-Red Stick commander.

The illegal treaty of 1825 was torn up. Menewa went to Washington and signed a new treaty whereby the Creeks were to keep their remaining 10,000,000 acres. As for Menewa himself, the chief gave his word that henceforth he would be loyal to the United States.

But the new treaty was only so much paper. The Creeks reeled under the waves of white squatters, land speculators, and bootleggers who invaded their country at this time. The state laws of Georgia and Alabama protected these thieves and criminals, and the Indians had no defense. Driven desperate, they at last accepted a removal treaty. One provision of it gave them comfort: they would have five years to get ready to go, and all the white intruders were to be cleared out at once so that during those five years the nation would not be troubled by them.

The Creeks did not stay comforted long. Instead of fewer intruders, they had more; instead of improving, their situation grew worse. Their crops and homes were taken away, and they were driven into the forests and swamps. Newspaper stories of the time give shocking pictures of their state—the whole people was starving. The incessant cry was *bread! bread!* Many ate roots and the bark of trees. Nothing was so bad that they would refuse to eat it. Haggard and naked, they begged their food from door to door.

The President and his Secretary of War were deaf to appeals. It was not that they *couldn't* do anything. They *wouldn't*. Clear the Indians out was administration policy. When four of the five treaty years were over, a resistance movement began among the Creeks. The Secretary of War immediately ordered an army into Alabama to subdue the Indians and remove the whole tribe to the West. Menewa himself, true to his promise of loyalty, helped to round up the rebellious Creeks.

The captured "hostiles" were started

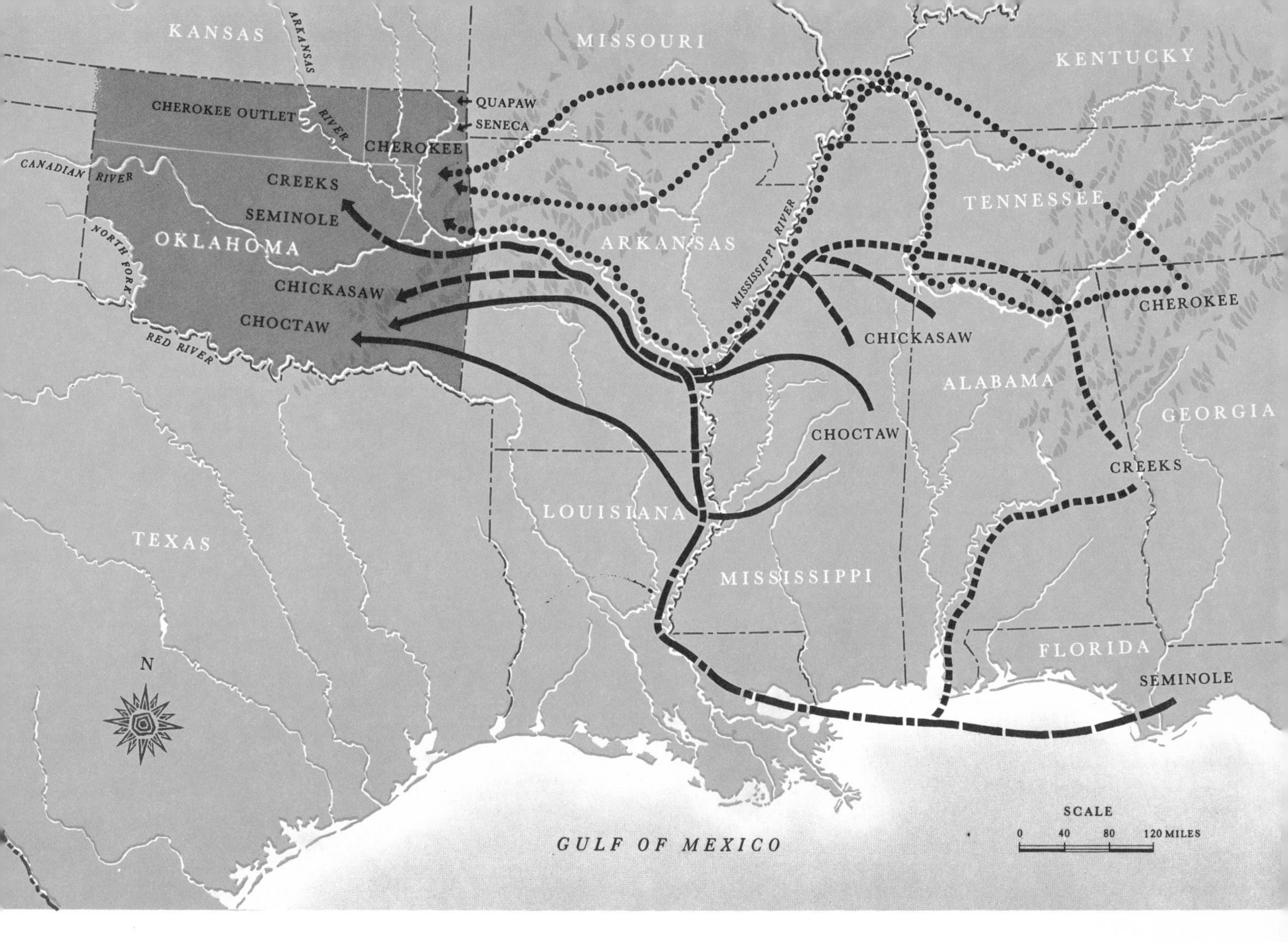

Removal routes of the five Civilized Tribes to Indian Territory.

west in a double-file procession, manacled and chained together. Their 84-year-old leader, Eneah Emathla, was among them. He never uttered a complaint.

Within a short period of their arrival in Indiana Territory, 3,500 of the 15,000 Creeks died of disease and exposure.

And so the nations departed. The Cherokees resisted year after year. They hung on, they bore every fraud and injustice, they made appeals. They pushed a legal fight until they won their case in the United States Supreme Court. Chief Justice Marshall blazingly denounced the wrongs done to the Indians by the state of Georgia, and the Supreme Court found the acts of the State of Georgia unconstitutional.

There was wild celebration in the Cherokee nation. But it all ended as they might well have known it would—President Jackson refused to carry out the decision of the court.

The Cherokees made one last appeal. This time they wrote to the Congress of the United States, and that document remains to shame Americans forever.

"In truth, our cause is your own," they said. "It is the cause of liberty and of justice. It is based upon your own principles, which we have learned from yourselves; for we have gloried to count your Washington and your Jefferson our great teachers. . . . We have practised their precepts with success. And the result is manifest. The wilderness of forest has given place to comfortable dwellings and cultivated fields. . . . Mental culture, industrial habits, and domestic enjoyments, have succeeded the rudeness of the savage state. We have learned your religion also. We have read your sacred books. Hundreds of our people have embraced their doctrines, practised the virtues they teach, cherished the hopes they awaken . . . we speak to the representatives of a Christian country; the friends of justice; the patrons of the oppressed. And our hopes revive, and our prospects brighten, as we indulge the thought. On your sentence our fate is suspended. . . . On your kindness, on your humanity, on your compassions, on your benevolence, we rest our hopes. . . ."

The Congress of the United States did nothing. In 1838 and 1839 the United States Army removed the Cherokee people by force.

On that "Trail of Tears" to the west, 4,600 of the nation perished. A few hundred Cherokees refused to submit. They hid in the mountains of North Carolina, and there their descendants live to this day.

Many Americans wanted the Seminoles of Florida, the fifth of the Civilized Nations, removed too. But an attempt to do it brought on a war which lasted seven years. That war cost the lives of 1,500 American troops and $20,000,000 in military expenses. For not one Seminole proved false to his country. Nor did a single first-rate warrior ever surrender. The high point of the war was, indeed, the capture of the young Seminole chief Osceola. But it was achieved by treachery, under a flag of truce.

Osceola died in a military prison three months afterward. The war went on without him. Seminole women killed their small children, as Creek women had done, to free themselves to fight beside their men. The war became a game of hide-and-seek in the swamps of the Florida Everglades. When it became clear that neither side could win, the United States called off the war.

Peace was made on quite honorable terms. Most of the Seminoles moved west to Indian Territory, but several bands remained in the region of the Everglades and are still there. Though many inducements have been offered them to emigrate, the Seminoles have refused them all.

MARK F. BOYD COLLECTION, UNIVERSITY OF MIAMI

The Seminole leader Osceola. Unable to capture him in battle, the Americans treacherously seized Osceola under a flag of truce.

LIBRARY OF CONGRESS

The fury of a Seminole attack on an American fort as depicted in 1837. Some of the Seminoles never surrendered, and their descendants still live in Florida.

Was anyone spared? Was any distinction made between friends and foes?

In the Southeast the story of the Northeast was repeated. The old faithful allies among the Creeks and Cherokees came off no better in the removal than the ancient hostile tribes. Those who had made possible the victory at Horseshoe Bend and had launched General Jackson on his national career had to leave just as did all the rest. Every promise made to every individual was broken. Menewa was given a personal promise from high authority that he could stay. Nevertheless he was forced to go. On the night before he left for exile, he went back to his town of Okfuskee and spent the night alone. He went to see the sun set for the last time, and its light shine upon the treetops, and the land, and the water that he was never to look upon again. Then he went back to take the westward trail. He was an old man and had many times been wounded. . . .

And so the nations were gone from their warm and charming land. Fifty thousand or so people had been uprooted. But something more had happened. The American people had been treated to quite a sight of dirty business. They had seen a people openly exploited in conspiracy involving the President of the United States. In short, a story of crime without punishment had been told, and it is reasonable to suppose that Young America drew the moral.

PUBLIC ARCHIVES OF CANADA

21. THE IMAGE MAKERS

As we have seen, the Europeans had a profound and cruelly destructive effect upon the Indians. Was it all one way? Or did the Indians in their turn affect the Old World? It might be well to pause in our story and examine this point.

When Columbus brought his first half-dozen Indians back with him to Spain, they created a sensation. Wherever the Admiral of the Ocean Fleet appeared, business stopped, bells were rung, streets were lighted with torches. The explorer, granted an extraordinary honor, sat in the presence of the king and queen, and his Indians ranked about his throne like wonder-bringing cherubim.

Spain opened wide its eyes. And after Spain, Europe. Wonders had arrived in the Old World from the New. From that time on, in a fairly real sense, they never ceased.

There were, in the first place, all the exciting new crops that had been developed by the Indians: maize, tomatoes, the common varieties of beans, white and sweet potatoes, squash and pumpkins, rubber, tobacco, long staple cotton, a long list of drugs including quinine and cocaine, and such delightful things as peanuts, popcorn, and chewing gum. All these worked fairly rapid changes in the Old World. Chocolate, brought from Mexico, became so popular in Spain that some people couldn't do without it even for an hour. Priests complained

Love among the Indians as it was not. A charming but unrealistic French lithograph.

COLLECTION OF PAUL WEATHERWAX; INDIANA UNIVERSITY, DEPT. OF BOTANY

The earliest known picture of corn to appear in Europe (1542). From a botany book by Leonhard Fuchs.

because worshipers brought chocolate to church and disturbed the services by sipping during Mass.

These were direct effects. In time they changed the food habits of the Old World. They affected agriculture, industry, commerce, health. They introduced new vices and new pleasures.

But there were also indirect effects. The smell of gold and spice and turquoise filled the nostrils of the first Spaniards in the New World. And yet, curiously, it is something else that most fills the first reports. Letter after letter speaks at great length of the peculiar character, the childlikeness, of the lovely people. The Spaniards could almost imagine that the beautiful island girls who came forth dancing and singing to welcome

them at Caribbean towns were dryads and wood nymphs.

This childlikeness of the Indians seized on the imagination of Europeans. It remained a living force long after the plunging swords had crumbled into rust. Something had been found that had been lost. Something had been rediscovered that, in the midst of sordid money-getting, men yearned for.

"Among these simple souls," one Peter Martyr wrote about the Indians in 1577, "a few clothes serve the naked. Weights and measures are not needful to such as know not the skill of craft and deceit and have not the use of pestiferous money. . . . So that if we shall not be ashamed to confess the truth, they seem to live in that golden world of which the old writers speak so much: wherein men lived simply and innocently without enforcement of laws, without quarreling judges . . . content only to satisfy nature."

A golden world. Simple and innocent living. People content to have no more than they needed. This childlikeness, this simplicity, this naturalness of the inhabitants of the New World enchanted Europe. It influenced one great thinker after another. In 1750 the Frenchman Jean Jacques Rousseau drew the thoughts together and set before the world his vision of the natural man, the noble savage, pure, simple, and above all free. "Man is born free, and everywhere he is in chains," Rousseau wrote. The words were gunpowder. They undermined the thrones of Europe and sent them crashing. In those simple words, inspired by reports about the Indians, the French Revolution was born.

This portrait of Four Bears, a handsome chief of the Missouri River Mandans, was painted by George Catlin in 1832.

On the other side of the ocean, about a hundred years later, a pioneer American anthropologist, Lewis Henry Morgan, decided to see for himself what Indian society was really like. So he made many visits to the reservations of the Iroquois. He didn't expect to see, and he didn't find, a golden world. But the peculiar character of the Indians made a great impression on him.

Here were human beings who didn't spend their lives acquiring property. Here were a people who weren't forever in competition against one another for personal gain. Instead of spending their time in piling up their own individual wealth, they spent their time in living. Morgan saw democracy in Iroquois government, where chiefs were chosen by the women and could be dismissed if they proved unsatisfactory. He saw brotherhood in Iroquois society, where land was owned in common. He saw equality in rights and privileges.

With a shock he compared this Indian society with his own, where each individual tried to get ahead of his neighbors at their expense. Was property so all-important? Was it the end and aim of life? Already man had created so much property that it had become an unmanageable power. "The human mind stands bewildered in the presence of its own creation," he wrote. "A mere property career is not the final destiny of mankind." And he, too, painted his vision of a different world. It would be a world based on the liberty, equality, and fraternity which he saw in Iroquois society. Only, of course, it would be on a higher level.

A German political writer, Friedrich Engels, picked up where Morgan left off. What an amazing government the Indians had! "No soldiers, no gendarmes or police, no nobles, kings, regents, prefects, or judges, no prisons, no lawsuits. . . . All are equal and free—the women included." As for the kind of men and women such a society bred, wasn't the admiration the Indians inspired proof enough? Weren't all white people who had come in contact with unspoiled Indians impressed by their dignity, uprightness, strength of character, and courage?

The idea which Europeans got of the Indian was often a far cry from reality. But the fact remains that the peculiar character of the Indian did actually affect Europeans. The white men who came to the New World after 1600 were already a little bit different from the men who had come a hundred years before. And at least some of that difference was due to the Indians they were coming to plunder and push aside.

Europeans in the New World often admired individual Indians very much. But the white men never hid the fact that they thought themselves superior. Didn't they know a thousand things in the field of mechanics that the Indians had no notion of? And the savages were so impractical! Instead of working and getting ahead, they occupied themselves with silly rituals and games and making pretty gew-gaws to wear in their hair. It was so childish, such a waste of good time that might have been spent working.

And yet the Indian way of life had a great appeal for those white men—and women—who tried it. During the colonial Indian wars, white captives often refused to leave their captors when they had the chance. Civilization didn't attract them once they had tasted freedom. With all its discomforts, they preferred the Indian way of life that had so little pressure in it. Why should a man work the fat off his back to acquire property when the twinkling stars were just as bright whether he worked or not? Living was better than getting.

This was something the European settlers couldn't understand. Why wouldn't the Indians work? Why didn't they want to labor to acquire things? It was frustrating to have them be so indolent. Here were colonizers having to ransack central Europe and the backwoods of Scotland and Ireland to find colonists whom they had to transport at great cost to America. And good, husky Indians were already right there on the spot. But just try to turn Indians into colonists. It couldn't be done—they wouldn't work.

Living, not getting. This peculiar quality, hidden in the image of the "noble savage," was the Indian's strength. But it was also his weakness. It was this that spelled his doom. This was the thing that destroyed the Indian nations. For living, not getting, made a gulf separating whites and Indians. Across the gulf there could be no understanding.

In the region that became the United States this gulf was at its widest and most unbridgeable. "Remember, that time is money," Benjamin Franklin wrote. It was hardly necessary to remind Americans of what they knew so well. Work and thrift were ingrained in them. Work was man's sacred calling. Everything was measured by the single yardstick of profit. Only if there was profit in it was a thing worth doing. To earn more and more money and strictly avoid all natural enjoyment—that was the guiding rule of life. The end and aim of everything was work leading to gain, to profit, to acquiring property.

In the light of such a rule, the Indian attitude was not only troublesome, it was downright immoral. Colonists of different

NEW-YORK HISTORICAL SOCIETY

A once proud Iroquois family, with two views of the wife, as sketched after the Revolution.

nationalities and various religions quarreled bitterly among themselves. But they were never so different from one another as from the Indians. The quarreling colonists could always make common cause against the Indians. For at bottom the Europeans were all after the very same thing—property.

It is true that frontiersmen often became more Indian than white in many ways. And this went deeper than simply using such gadgets as snowshoes and canoes. But they never forgot that the real object of their life was to get property. And this view was so different from the Indian view that the two could never hope to be members of the same club.

Spain, in general, was far more tolerant and made much more use of the Indian peoples. Large numbers of them were taken into the population of Spanish colonies. Indeed, this went on so much that what we today call Latin or Spanish America could almost as well be called Indian America. In Protestant North America nothing of that sort happened. The Indian nations were deliberately stamped out. They were stamped out to the point that the Indian race became the Vanishing American. At the same time, the stamping out was obscured so that many people didn't realize it was happening. To their minds the Indian was the Vanishing American not because he was being stamped out but because some secret natural law was operating on him. The Indian, they thought, just naturally withered away at the touch of civilization—as though it were a killing disease.

To those who hated violence and didn't want to think they were a party to the stamping out, this was a very comforting thought. But we know that there was no secret natural law acting to turn the Indian into the Vanishing American. Living, not

MERCALDO ARCHIVES

An engraving that perpetuated the image of the Indian as the savage redskin.

ROYAL ONTARIO MUSEUM

Salmon-spearing by torchlight on the Fox River in Wisconsin. Painted by a Canadian artist.

getting, was at the bottom of it.

As the white men drove the Indians away or exterminated them, the image of the noble savage changed. It was necessary to find a comforting reason for making the Indian vanish. So he became the bloodthirsty savage, reeking with gore. Town-dwelling Indians, rich in culture and cornfields, were made to appear in people's minds as wandering hunters, somewhat dirtier and less desirable than gypsies. And this, of course, made it easier to drive them away, or shoot them if they objected. Well-meaning citizens—good people—had to keep reminding themselves that the Creeks or the Sauks and Foxes who were robbed of their lands were just savages.

At the same time Americans were hungry for heroes. And who could fill the bill better than some of the Indians who had got into the news and become celebrities? There was Black Hawk, the Sauk and Fox leader, for instance. After his capture at the end of the "war" in 1832, he was taken on a triumphal tour of the cities of the East. And after his death his bones were stolen and exhibited for so much a look.

People found Indian heroes in fact as well as in the stories of Fenimore Cooper. The young, dashing, and courageous Petalesharo, chief of the Skidi (Wolf) Pawnees, made a sensation in Washington during his visit there in 1821. The Pawnee tribe had moved up from the Southeast to Nebraska but had kept up some of its temple-mound ceremonies. Once a year at the time of the summer solstice the rites came to a climax in a human sacrifice, Petalesharo put a stop to the practice—so it was reported—by rescuing a Comanche girl who was about to be sacrificed. It was all very dramatic and exciting and done in the best last-minute tradition. So Washington made a huge to-do about Petalesharo.

It was hard for people to get a clear idea of what the Indian was really like because he appeared in so many and such different images. Sometimes he was made out to be wondrous wise, sometimes he was romantic, then again he was the natural man, or he was the bloodthirsty savage. But as the Vanishing American vanished out of the eastern states, one image predominated. The Indian became a phantom. A warm, affectionate glow surrounded this phantom. It

LIBRARY OF CONGRESS

Petalesharo, young, dashing chief of the Skidi (Wolf) Pawnee, was one of the romantic Indian heroes of the mid-nineteenth century. He put a stop to human sacrifice as part of the temple-mound religious ceremonies of his tribe. A portrait of him, of which the above is a lithograph, was made by Charles Bird King.

LIBRARY OF CONGRESS

The death of Minnehaha from Longfellow's Song of Hiawatha. *A Currier and Ives lithograph.*

was the kind of affection we feel for someone who is dying. Affection poured out toward the phantom in a thousand poems. People took to their hearts Longfellow's Hiawatha and shed warm tears over the death of Minnehaha. People grew sadly thoughtful as they read the poems of Lydia Sigourney, "The Sweet Singer of Hartford," who pointed out to them that the vanished Indian had left his name on the waters and the hills:

> Ye say that all have passed away,
> The noble race and brave
> That their light canoes have vanished
> From off the crested wave;
> That 'mid the forests where they roamed,
> There rings no hunter's shout;
> But their name is on your waters,
> Ye may not wash it out . . . .
> Ye say their cone-like cabins
> That cluster o'er the vale
> Have disappeared as withered leaves
> Before the autumn gale:
> But their memory liveth on your hills . . . .

Sympathy, affection, yes. But understanding, no. The gulf remained, and all the jumbled images couldn't bridge it. They couldn't make the white man understand the Indians as people to be taken seriously, as people who were part of the national history and the national life. In spite of all the poetry and the tears, the practical American people understood only that it was necessary to remove the Civilized Tribes.

It was very sad and not quite legal, but really it had to be done. There was feeling for the Civilized Tribes when they were removed. The long and heroic resistance by the Creeks and Cherokees won admiration. But even the most indignant people couldn't see the other side of the tragedy. They never stopped to think how much the states of Georgia, Alabama, and Mississippi lost when they drove out people who could have been such superior citizens.

"Why should you take by force from us that which you can obtain by love?" Old Powhatan had asked.

But the Indians were gone and only the phantoms remained. Phantoms looked from the Alabama hill that broke Menewa's heart. Phantoms danced a solemn step or two in the busy streets of Plymouth, among the phantom lodges of Patuxet. Phantoms grinned at phantom jokes in a thousand phantom councils. Phantoms settled down to live in the names of the land, as the Sweet Singer said.

Creek Indians, armed with hatchets, bows and arrows, and rifles, rush to defend their village against American soldiers. After their defeat, many of the Creeks fled to Florida.

22. BEYOND THE MISSISSIPPI

In the meantime the real Indians, most of them, were jumbled west of the Mississippi. The exiles came to start life over. And from Texas to the high plains of the Missouri and on northward, the story began again. That story would not be so great a force as it had been. From now on the Indians would not influence history as they had done. But now they were to produce the most stirring images of all.

The nations beyond the Mississippi were, most of them, made up of people who lived a life similar in some ways to that of the eastern woodlands and in other ways like that of the great plains farther west. Along the eastern edge were the villages of such farmer-hunters as the Caddo, Omaha, and the Osage, makers of the famous bow of Osage orange that came from their country. Here, too, were the Oto, the Ponca, Quapaw, Wichita, and those other nations which would give their names to the states of Iowa, Kansas, and Missouri. The Kansa were familiar along the Santa Fe Trail where their men could always be recognized by their haircut—the head shaved or plucked except for one lock at the back. As for the Missouri, they were almost destroyed in a war with the Sauk and Foxes in 1798. Then soon afterward they were defeated by the Osage. That ended the Missouri as an independent tribe. Those who were left went to live with the Oto and Iowa.

North and west up the Missouri River began the country of the Sioux, the various divisions of the Dakota. But far up the Missouri, deep in the short-grass plains of modern North Dakota, were three tribes of village people who clung stubbornly to their own ways. They lived in earth-mound houses and raised their food in the rich bottom land of the upper Missouri. These were the Arikara, the Hidatsa, and the Mandan. They were very well known to early fur trappers, traders, and explorers. Especially the handsome and hospitable Mandan. For the Mandan were the middlemen of the Northern plains. They bought European goods from the white men and traded them to the other Indians. Their craftsmen produced beautiful leather work and the only pottery in the region, both much-wanted articles of trade. And the Mandan sold, besides, things that they raised because they grew more than they needed of maize, beans, pumpkins, and sunflower seed.

The trading Mandan were the most powerful of the farming tribes west of the Mississippi. At one time they had nine villages of roomy, high-domed lodges made of poles covered with sod. But in 1837 these Indians vanished suddenly because of a smallpox epidemic. Almost overnight their numbers shrank from 1,600 to perhaps 150 or less.

West of the farming nations were still others. To Lewis and Clark, making their famous exploring journey to the Sea of the West in 1804 to 1806, the tribes across the plains and mountains seemed endless. Each

SMITHSONIAN INSTITUTION

This roomy earthen Mandan lodge was not only a home but a stable and kennel as well. Squatting around the central fire, the men whiled away the time between hunts in smoking, mending their weapons, and boasting of their accomplishments.

had its own territory, each had its own way of life. Lewis and Clark met the differing people all the way. The explorers were in fact guided by one of those distant people, a Shoshoni girl from the Rocky Mountains named Sacagawea. Like Malinal, Sacagawea can never be forgotten. Nor is it likely that she will be, for there are said to be more statues dedicated to her than to any other woman in American history.

For the most part, the region between the Mississippi and the Rockies was unstable. Tribes came and went. Some split up into smaller groups on account of feuds or simply because they were restless and wanted to go their own way. Others mingled with strangers to form new tribes. But all the farming Indians west of the Mississippi were part-time hunters. They not only pursued the local game but trekked many miles to hunt the buffalo of the High Plains.

Before the coming of the horse, hunting the buffalo was a dangerous business. The hunters stalked the huge beasts on foot and were ever in danger of being trampled. Tricks of all sorts were resorted to. When the Indians learned that the buffalo weren't afraid of wolves, they used animal disguises. They would creep up to a herd under wolf skins. Often sentries were posted for miles. At a signal they waved robes and shouted to stampede the buffalo over cliffs or into corrals. Sometimes the

Indians set the dry prairie grass on fire to start the buffalo moving.

In those early days the dog was the Indians' beast of burden. On every journey dogs dragged whatever had to be taken along. Two tipi poles were tied to the dog's shoulders. The free ends dragged along the ground and across them the baggage was lashed. This contraption, named a travois by the French Canadians, did duty as a wagon. The dog and the travois were indispensable in buffalo hunting. They carried home the dried buffalo meat and the hides.

The horse changed everything west of the Mississippi. The manner of hunting the buffalo was immediately transformed. Mounted on his trained buffalo pony, which seemed to enjoy the hunt as much as the rider, the hunter could pick out the choicest cows in the milling herd without fear of being trampled. He had all the advantage in speed. On horseback, moreover, the long trek to and from the hunting grounds was cut by weeks. Far longer journeys could be undertaken. And with horses instead of dogs pulling the travois, far bigger loads of meat and hides could be taken home. Tribe after tribe forsook agriculture for hunting. The buffalo became the center of their lives.

The buffalo seemed to the Indians to be a gift from the Creator. The mighty herds which moved like dark living seas across the rolling plains gave the Indians everything they needed. Buffalo flesh was their food. Dried and pounded up with suet, marrow, and wild cherries, the meat became pemmican, a nourishing food, and one that would keep indefinitely. Buffalo hides made the Indians' tipis, their clothing, the warm covering for their beds. It made their saddles and shields. The sinews of the buffalo made their bowstrings. Moccasins, leggings, bags—all were sewn with buffalo sinew. Shoulder bones were turned into hoes, rib bones became runners for dog sleds. The porous hip bones did duty as paint brushes. From the horns the Indians made spoons and cups and bowls. The hoofs yielded them glue. Even buffalo chips, the dried dung of the buffalo, didn't go to waste. On the treeless plains buffalo chips became the Indians' fuel.

The buffalo was a miracle. But the horse seemed even more so. After all, the buffalo had always been there while the horse was new. Many things took on bigger proportions west of the Mississippi because of the horse. Lodge poles could now be as long as 30 feet, for horses could drag them when the time came to move. Tipis could be made of as many as 40 buffalo hides. Home could be a roomy place crammed with furnishings, riches, and relations. Horses would carry everything.

Speed, comfort, the certainty of food, and a greater dignity to life all around—these things the horse brought to the Indians. By the early 1700s all the tribes around the buffalo country had horses. And when the white men found these Indians, they seemed born to ride.

Spectators watch the Bull Society Dance from the rooftops of a Mandan village. This dance was a wild ceremony meant to draw the buffalo herds closer to the village. The handsome, genial, hospitable Mandan were very well known to early fur trappers, traders, and explorers along the upper Missouri. They farmed and grew bumper crops of corn, selling what they did not need to other tribes. They worked leather beautifully and made the only pottery in the region. In 1837 the Mandan vanished almost overnight when a smallpox epidemic all but wiped them out. Of 1,600 persons only thirty-one were left.

BRITISH MU

Eskimos of Baffin Island, Canada, attacking English sailors. This 1577 scene is presumed to have been painted by John White, who later made paintings and drawings of North Carolina natives and towns.

23. KAYAKERS

In 1848 the eyes of the world turned on the land of the Eskimo. Sir John Franklin and his expedition to the Arctic had disappeared and a search was on. Thirty-eight expeditions went out in the next ten years. By the time it was learned that the explorers had all died of starvation, the Eskimo had become a familiar figure to Americans. Whalers, of course, and fur traders and missionaries had known him for 200 years before this time. But now the fur-clad Eskimo of the Far North with his igloo, his dog sled, and his kayak was firmly fixed in everybody's mind.

The Eskimo is a newcomer among the American peoples. But even so he has been in his Arctic homeland at least for 2,500 years, if not a good deal longer. For there were people in the Far North 5,000 to 8,000 years ago who may have been his ancestors.

Eskimos have an Asiatic look about them but are a type unto themselves. Though they come of the same stock as the Indians, they made their appearance in the New World much later. They do not regard themselves as Indians. They call themselves Inuit, which is to say The People. But many Indian nations call themselves The People. Eskimos' language is a complete mystery—it seems to be unrelated to any other language on earth. But this, again, can be said of many Indian languages.

Time was when the Eskimos were the only sign of man for a swing of 5,000 miles across the Arctic and sub-Arctic. From Siberia across Alaska and the vast reaches of northern Canada to Greenland their villages were the only human habitations. But there were never many Eskimos. In all this immense country there were probably at most 50,000 to 100,000 people.

They had no tribal governments and no village governments. So they had no wars. They had no law except custom and taboo. The family itself did all the governing. If somebody was murdered, it was up to the victim's relatives to do the punishing.

And yet, for all that they had neither laws nor government to unite them, the Eskimos were one. Except for the Aleuts (pronounced Alley-oots) of the Aleutian Islands, they all spoke very similar dialects and did things much the same way. What is more, they stayed the same through the long centuries. You would have to compare the work of their hands a thousand years apart to see any change in it.

On the coast the Eskimos hunted the whale, the walrus, and the seal. Inland they hunted the caribou. Which way of life came first nobody can say. Nor does anyone know whether the Eskimo way of life came *from* Asia or spread back *to* Asia. The famous snow house has never been seen in Asia, so that, at least, must be an Eskimo invention of the New World. But what about the other ingenious things that are part of Eskimo life?

As far back as we know the Eskimos, they already had nearly all the familiar things. They had boats made of skins sewed over wooden frames—both the one-man kayak

MUSEUM OF THE AMERICAN INDIAN, HEYE FOUNDATION

Eskimo masks, like this one from Alaska representing the swan that drives whales to the hunter, have the fragile quality of mobiles.

and the larger umiak. They had sleds with runners of bone or ivory to use with dogs. They had ivory snow goggles with holes or slits in them. They had hobnails of bone or ivory for lashing to boot soles in working their way over ice. Ice scoops and ice picks; plugs to stop up wounds of animals and save the precious blood; special harpooning gear, special bird-catching gear; bows and arrows for hunting musk ox, caribou, and other big game—all these they had. And usually they had the seal-oil lamp, the only lamp known in the Americas. It consisted of a saucer of oil in which floated a wick of moss. At first this was used only for light. Later on it was used for heat and cooking. In areas where there was no wood, this oil lamp was the only heat—and this in a land where the temperature could settle down and stay for a while at 50 or 60 degrees below zero.

We can picture the people, but it is hard to picture the life with its long, dark winters, the terrible cold, the hardships, and danger. Strangely, this difficult, anxious life didn't make a disagreeable people of the Eskimos. On the contrary, they are usually described as placid and rather jolly. It is no wonder they were inventive—they had to be to survive. The wonder is that, living in that harsh world, they had time and thought for art. In the centuries between A.D. 1 and 1000, they did beautiful bone and ivory carving and engraving. Some of the best was reserved for the dead. Reposing in their log tombs, the dead were furnished with artificial eyes of inlaid ivory. They had mouth covers and nose plugs of carved ivory, and elaborate ivory masks. Carved animal figures, carved ivory spirals and chains were also placed in the tombs.

The central Eskimos say that at one time another race lived among them, a mighty race with mighty ancestors. They were men so powerful that one of them alone could haul a walrus across the ice as easily as an Eskimo could drag a seal. The people were known as the Tunit. For some reason they went away. There are reasons to believe that the Tunit were a real, not an imaginary people, yet who they were or where they went nobody knows.

After A.D. 1000 the ancient way of life changed in many respects. But it changed slowly. It wasn't till the 1700s that pipes and tobacco reached the Far North. And they didn't come up from the south. Tobacco traveled all the way around the world and reached the Eskimos by way of Siberia. Changes came, yet for the most part living remained the same. Summer houses were usually skin tents. Winter dwellings depended on what was available—driftwood, whalebones, sod, stone, or snow. In Alaska the domed snow house was rare. Canada was the place for that, and modern explorers have visited halls of snow roomy enough for dancing parties of 60 people. Skylights were paned with stretched walrus gut. But whatever the house was like, the principal piece of furniture in it was the drying frame. Clothes were constantly getting wet.

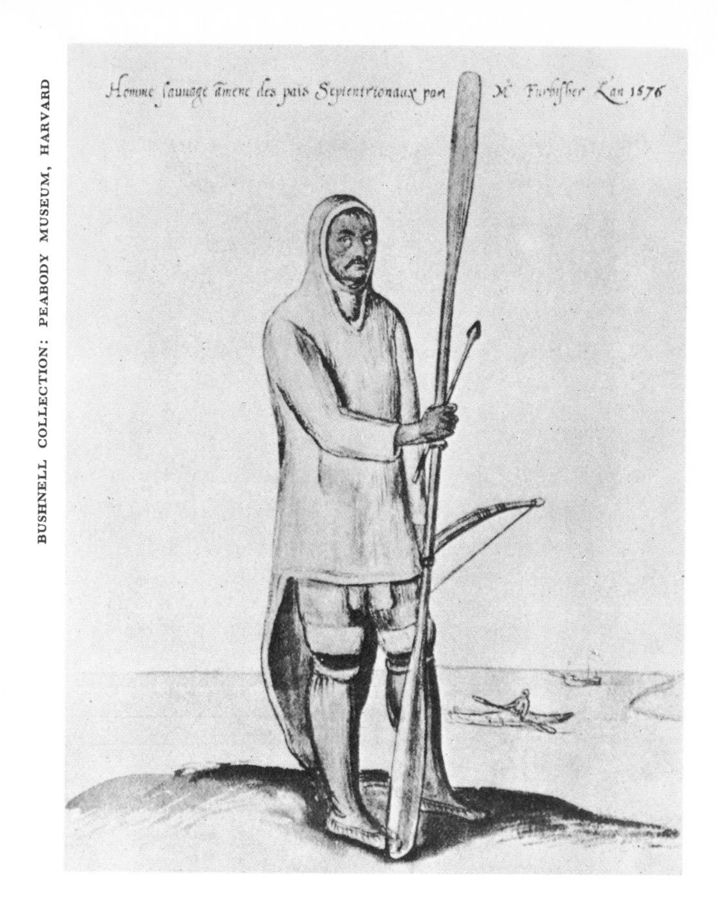

BUSHNELL COLLECTION: PEABODY MUSEUM, HARVARD

This sketch, which was made in 1576, is the earliest known picture of an Eskimo.

In the winter the Eskimos hunted seals at the ice edge or breathing holes. This was a freezing job—they had to wait motionless for hours with harpoon ready. In the spring, seals were hunted as they basked on the shores. In the summer, they were harpooned from kayaks in the open sea. Kayakers became wonderfully expert at handling their peculiar craft, in which man and boat are one. But even so, Arctic waters are wild and dangerous, and it is not surprising that one of the Eskimo words to travel farthest among neighboring people is *pivoq*. It means "he lost his life by upsetting in his kayak."

In the summer the whalers put out in their umiaks. And where there were no whales, whole villages moved inland to hunt the caribou.

Like the Indians throughout the Americas, the Eskimos believed the world could be easily thrown out of balance. If there was illness, misfortune, or lack of game, the reason was always the same—somebody had done something wrong. A shaman would find out what had gone wrong and correct it.

Had the sick woman's husband perhaps speared a salmon at the time when it was restricted? Then of course the salmon were indignant and wouldn't let themselves be caught. Or perhaps a sin had floated down to the bottom of the sea and fallen like dirt in the hair of the great goddess She Down There. Then of course she was indignant and was keeping the fat creatures of the sea out of reach. The shaman would have to make a spirit journey down to her and square things.

The shaman was common among many Indians, but particularly popular among the Eskimos. Women could be shamans as well as men, maybe better. They performed magic, got revenge, cured illness. Sometimes they cured by a method very widely known in both Americas. They would suck out the illness and spit out a pebble or some such object to prove it.

The ages passed and the Eskimos did all the same age-old things through the brief summers and the long winters of night when they harnessed their sled dogs by the green light of the aurora. Life was always and everywhere hard. But it was hardest for the inland Eskimos, the caribou hunters. For them winter was only another name for hunger.

There were Indians inhabiting the Far North as well as Eskimos. They lived inland in the great black spruce forests south of the treeless tundra. And they, too, knew starving times. These Indian tribes were the Naskapi in Labrador, the Cree and

Chipewyan around Hudson Bay, and various wandering Athapascan groups. The Athapascans of the Far North are still strangers to us. We know less about them than any other Indians in North America. They live all across northwest Canada from Hudson Bay almost to the Pacific, and there are 21 main tribes of them. Some were given their name by traders and are known as Yellowknives (because they had knives of copper), Dog-ribs (because they claimed descent from dogs), and Slaves (because other tribes looked down on them). The Beaver and Hare were named for their

SEATTLE MUSEUM OF HISTORY AND INDUSTRY

This drawing in ink on reindeer skin was made by a present-day Alaskan native artist, George Aghupuk. It shows many activities of Eskimo life, ranging from daily chores of cooking to occasions for celebration or recreation, when a circle forms for singing and dancing. The caribou trappers at upper left, the seal stalkers at lower left, and the ice fisherman at lower right display several of the hunting methods practiced by the Alaskans.

favorite game. The Carriers got their name because it was a custom of that tribe for a widow to carry the ashes of her husband for three years in a basket.

The life of the inland Indians living in the northern forests was on the whole harder than that of the Eskimos. After all, only a few Eskimos lived inland and depended on the undependable caribou. Most drew a rich harvest from the sea. Their life was indeed rugged and dangerous. But they had adapted themselves to it and until the white men brought them "civilization" they were content.

Totem poles at Alert Bay, Vancouver Island. Two represent the thunderbird and bear mother.

A huge seagoing Kwakiutl canoe, in the prow of which stands a man dressed as a thunderbird.

24. POTLATCHERS AND CANNIBAL DANCERS

Usually it is farming and pottery-making people who build a high culture. On the Northwest Coast the nations did neither of these things and yet they made great progress. Moreover, they got far without any help from Mexico and points south. Their ways and ideas were closer to Asia.

All this was a marvel in the New World. And so was the attitude about property. Unlike most Indians, the people of the Northwest Coast placed great value on property. And they accumulated it mainly for purposes of display.

Theirs was a sea-and-river way of life, for they fed largely on fish—salmon, cod, and halibut. Roots and berries from the lush rain forests of the coast gave variety to this fish diet. Camas root—sweet bulbs of the lily family—was the chief vegetable food. Cranberries, blueberries, and the saskatoon berry, which contains three times as much iron and copper as prunes and raisins, filled in. Food was plentiful and easy to get. Work in the spring and summer laid up enough for the year. So the mild winters were free. They could be used for pleasure and for the creation of beautiful things. The pleasure was mainly ceremonials of the clans and secret societies, though some of the most exciting winter events had to do with social climbing. As for art, it was a wealth of decorated blankets, baskets, boxes, and wood and stone carving.

Families that were related lived together in gabled plank houses. Here was where the fantastic carving began. The house posts and door poles were carved and painted with the family crest. And out of this developed the famous totem poles that came to stand in front of the dwellings. The word *totem* means "family" or "clan."

Seagoing people naturally become skilled makers of vessels. The people of the Northwest Coast were famous for their mighty canoes that measured 60 feet. They hollowed them out of a single log by fire and adze and then carved fanciful figures on them. White men who knew the skills of the sea and saw the Indians maneuver such monster canoes said they handled them remarkably well. Some peoples showed great daring in the waters. The Nootka of Vancouver Island used their barbaric longboats for whaling by a method that called for the greatest courage. They harpooned the whale again and again and finally killed it with a thrusted lance, then towed the creature to shore.

In their warfare, slat armor and wooden helmets were used, and possibly carved masks to terrify the enemy. Slave raids were common. Indeed, they were so common that in some of the rich villages one-third of the people were slaves. An American captive in the early 1800s reported that a Nootka chief had "nearly fifty male and female slaves." Slaves were grand to show off with. A chief who was building a new house might have a slave killed and buried with the sinking of the first house-post. Or the chief might have the canoe of a visitor dragged up onto the beach over the bodies of slaves especially killed for that purpose.

It is a mistake to think of the Indians as a stolid, self-contained people. Many Indians are emotional. Certainly those of the Northwest Coast were given to weeping and exaggerated ways of behaving. Also, they had a lot of imagination. Mighty spirits walked the earth—at least in the tales told in winter when the North wind blew. The stories were terrifying. "Something wonderful came in and stood there. His large eyelids were too powerful to look at. Where he placed his foot he stood for a while. When he took another step the earth and the house shook. . . ."

The culture of the Northwest Coast started with the Tlingit far up along the southernmost reaches of Alaska and stretched all the way down to northern California. In that long strip the ways of doing things varied a good deal, naturally. The Tlingit and Tsimshian people were famous, among other things, for their Chilkat blanket. This was made from cedar bark and the hair of the wild mountain goat, and into it was woven a mystic design that had the power of speech. So they said. The Haida and Kwakiutl did the best wood carving. The Tsimshian were traders. They dealt in copper from the north and captured Salishan slaves from the south. They traded otter skins from the Haida and dentalium shells—a sort of wampum—and candlefish oil from anywhere. (The candlefish is so oily that when it is dried it can be used as a candle.)

The nations had different names, though most of them meant the same thing—People. For they spoke varying languages. But the Chinook tongue of the Columbia River region was the language of trade, just as Choctaw was the language of trade along the Gulf Coast. In time Chinook came to be spoken from California to Alaska. But, oddly enough, the Chinook themselves merged with another tribe and dropped their own language entirely.

It is the Chinook trade language that gave us the word *potlatch*. Potlatch really means "giving." But it came to mean a feast given to celebrate any sort of occasion. Often it might be a coming-out party for a debutante daughter. At this feast extravagant gifts were given away—blankets, cedar chests, sea-otter furs. But this was only the start. The occasion called for as much showing off as possible, so there was a great waste of wealth, all of which gave prestige to the potlatch giver. Of course, when one chief showed off, the chief of a rival clan had to show off too, and go him one better. So potlatches became contests in waste, which was the best way of proving how rich a chief was and how he scorned it all. Precious oil would be thrown on the fire until guests were singed by the flames. A wealthy chief would kill a valuable slave with a special club known as a "slave killer" and fling the slave's scalp to his rival. Or he would break and destroy an even more valuable "copper." This was a plate of wrought copper that was used as money, and to destroy it was about equal to lighting a cigar with a $1,000 bill. All the gift giving was carried out with great formality, and the rival clan leaders sang songs of

The foreboding wooden mask at the right represents a sea monster. It was used in Kwakiutl ceremonies on the Northwest Coast.

MUSEUM OF THE AMERICAN INDIAN, HEYE FOUNDATION

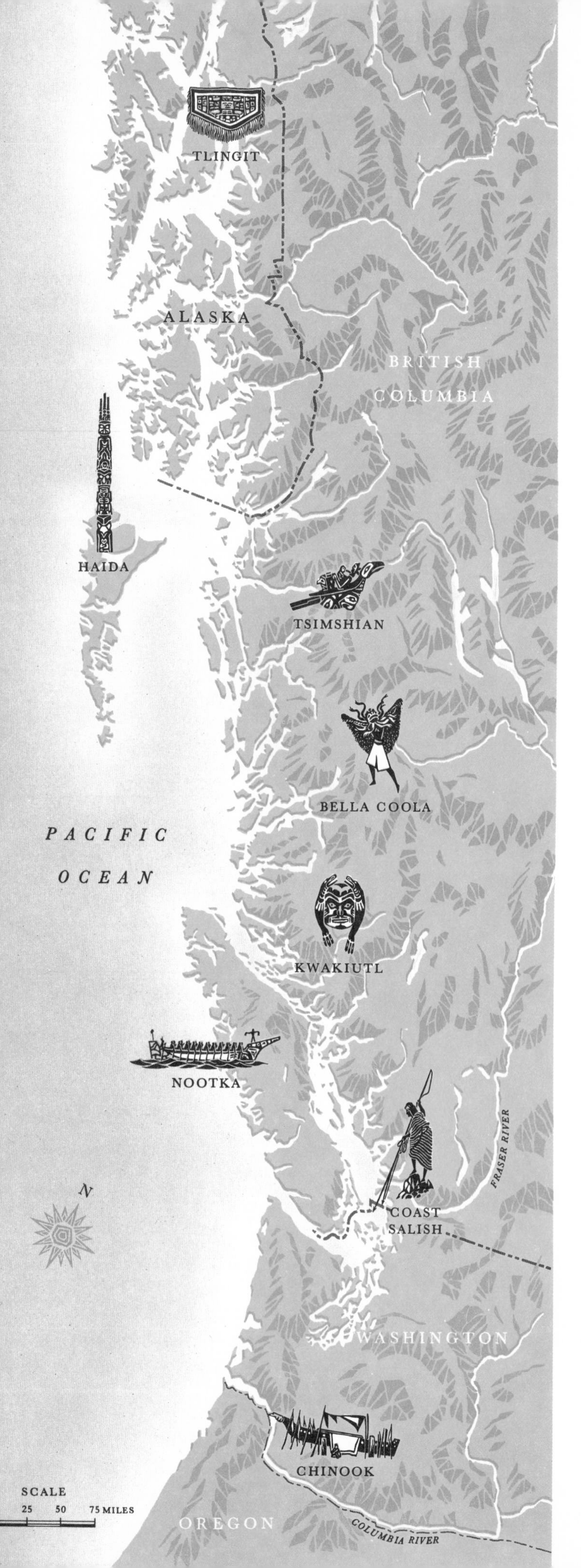

insult to each other:

"What will my rival say again—that 'spider woman,' what will he pretend to do next? . . . Will he not brag that he is going to give away canoes, that he is going to break coppers? . . . This I throw into your face . . ."

Such behavior in our society would be called abnormal, but on the Northwest Coast it was the usual thing. Among the Kwakiutl, to glorify yourself and ridicule your rivals was the object of every undertaking. And the one unbearable thing was shame!

The rival who was outshone sometimes couldn't stand the humiliation. He would sail off to war and deliberately throw away his life. What is more important, the entire clan won or lost face along with their chief. So the whole clan labored to make the really grand potlatches possible. They were a spur to industry. Many beautiful things were made just in order that a chief might give them away or destroy them. Among the Kwakiutl the pace of making things was particularly stepped up. For among them the custom was that at the next potlatch twice as much had to be given away as at the one before.

Thoughts about property filled the minds of the people of the Northwest Coast. Property was something with which one could shame one's rivals and establish one's own superiority. Property was a defense against shame; so preoccupied, indeed, was the Northwest Coast with property that even intangible things were reckoned as property and could be handed down. As the people were divided into nobles and commoners, titles could be inherited. The right to be a carver or a boatbuilder was inherited. Ownership of certain songs or dances was inherited.

Map shows the approximate homelands of the Northwest coastal peoples.

Young men and women of many Indian nations went alone into the forest to fast and pray and seek a vision to guide them. But on the Northwest Coast the right to do so was also one of the things that was inherited, for you inherited the right to belong to a secret society, and this was part of it. It gave you great prestige to belong to a secret society. It also brought the highest excitement. In the secret societies you took part in rites that went back to the very dawn of man. The cult of the Bear and the cult of the Cannibal came to the Northwest Coast out of the mists of time, and to take part in those ceremonies was more hair-raising than anything else on the Northwest Coast.

The people thrilled to the rites of these cults. Their hearts thumped fearfully as the Bear dancer danced and juggled glowing coals, throwing them among the onlookers, setting their bark clothes on fire. Meantime the Bears of the Bear Society, wrapped in their great black bearskins, angrily clawed the earth. And the people sang:

> How shall we hide from the bear that is
>   moving all around the world? . . .
> Let us cover our backs
>   with dirt that the terrible great
>   bear from the north of the world may
>   not find us . . .

The youth who was being initiated into the Kwakiutl Cannibal Society had a dreadful ordeal to go through. Before he appeared for the dance of initiation, he had to fast in the woods for days. Then, wasted and hysterical, he came out. A dancing woman went out to meet him. In her outstretched arms she carried a corpse. Dancing backward, she lured him to the house of the Society. Step for step he followed her, trembling, drawn on as if against his will. In the house he was seized with wildness. He bit flesh from the arms of those who were taking part in the ceremony. And, carried away with emotion, he danced while the people sang for him:

> Now I am about to eat,
> My face is ghastly pale.
> I am about to eat what was given me by
>   Cannibal at the North End of the World.

He didn't really eat the corpse. The ceremony ended with a feast of dog. Dog was the usual stand-in for man in the mock-cannibal rites among a number of Indian peoples.

The right to go through such terrors was, as we said, inherited. But anyone could see spirits in secret dreams, and the spirits could be prayed to. Toward the southern end of the Northwest Coast world this spirit dreaming was of great importance. Young dreamers went deep into the towering forests of Douglas fir or redwood to pray. And it is not surprising that, with all the devotion of their hearts, they prayed: "I want to be rich."

Tlingit charm, carved from ivory

MUSEUM OF THE AMERICAN INDIAN, HEYE FOUNDATION

25. "CIVILIZATION" COMES TO THE FAR NORTH

It was the fur trade that brought "civilization" to the people of the Far North, Indians and Eskimos alike. And the first thing they got was liquor. Hundreds of gallons found their way north while rival companies fought for furs. New diseases also came with the white man and, as usual, took their toll. They consumed the people of the northern forests "as the fire consumes the dry grass of the fields."

But the deepest changes were of another kind. The Indians and Eskimos were transformed from hunters to trappers. No longer did they center their life around the caribou and seal. They had no time for hunting—summer had to be spent trading, not storing up a winter meat supply. Besides, the caribou were now very few anyway. For the white men had caused them to be butchered by the herd for their hides. From some parts of their range the caribou had vanished altogether. Now the winter food of the one-time hunters was flapjacks, made out of flour got at the Hudson's Bay Company stores.

Whalers also invaded the country of the north. They came year after year so regularly that the Polar Eskimos called them *upernagdlit*, "harbingers of spring." Many came from New Bedford in Massachusetts.

Thompson River fur-trade Indian

Nootka native with nose ornament

BOTH: PROVINCIAL ARCHIVES, VICTORIA

The vessels plowed the northern waters of Hudson Bay and often had Eskimos as crews.

In the west, in the Aleutians and Alaska, civilization came by way of Russian fur traders led by Siberian frontiersmen. They had absolutely no regard for life. They slew whatever they found on the beaches—seals, the six-foot Bering Sea king crabs, or the "mild, polite, and hospitable" Aleuts.

The Russian Czar put a stop to this freebooting. In 1799 he gave exclusive fur rights in the New World to the newly formed Russian American Company. But by the time this happened only a tenth of the Aleuts were left. The Russians made an effort to look after the survivors. Missionaries came and converted the people to the Greek Orthodox Church. Tradition says they joined to a man, saying, "Any religion which can save the Russians must be very strong."

The Aleuts were put to work hunting the valuable sea-otter and, under Russian command, voyaged as far south as Santa Barbara in southern California. Eighty Aleuts helped colonize a Russian trading post in northern California. Then the Russians set up a fort at Sitka on Tlingit territory.

To the Spaniards in the New World all these Russian activities seemed a threat, so now they hurried to get their share of the trade. In 1773 and 1774 they made a trip up the northwest coast to Alaska. After that Spanish, English, and then American ships kept coming up to Nootka Sound on Vancouver Island. They traded with the Nootka and very quickly got in trouble with them. After several massacres and the destruction of a couple of Yankee vessels, the whale-hunting Nootka got quite a reputation for toughness. At the same time they

PROVINCIAL ARCHIVES, VICTORIA

When trading on European vessels, Indians like the Nootka above wore formal "button blankets" ornamented with pearl shells.

got something else—steel tools, just what they needed for their wood carving. The carving art of the northwest coast flamed into a most glorious sunburst.

But the sunburst was a sunset. For the Russians now seemed a threat to England and the United States, and soon English and American trading posts were springing up on the lower Columbia River. Then missionaries came into Oregon, and after them settlers. With that the world of the northwest coast, its potlatches and its social climbers, started on the way down.

In 1853, when war broke out in the Crimea, the Russians became anxious about their "possessions" in far-off America. It would be better, they decided, to sell Alaska before the British got their hands on it.

So they started dickering with the United States, and the sale finally went through for $7,200,000. It was a bargain. Ninety-four times the amount has since been taken out in gold alone.

On October 18, 1867, Alaska changed hands. American officials and American troops came ashore at Sitka and took over. The steamer that brought them also brought a Baltimore businessman who did a little business that day with some of the Russian sealing company people. Back in San Francisco he helped organize the Alaska Commercial Company. The name sounded innocent enough. But what the company did on the Pribilof Islands was not innocent.

The Pribilof Islands are a group of barren islands famous for seals. Here every summer all the fur seals of the eastern Pacific come to breed. In 1870 the rights to these priceless seal fisheries were granted to the Alaska Commercial Company for 20 years. During that time the company netted many millions of dollars. But in its greed it almost wiped out the vast seal herds. Nor, according to missionaries, did it improve the lot of the Aleuts who lived on the Pribilof Islands, though the company claimed it had done so. Congress tried to get at the truth and got nowhere. For the United States agent who was supposed to protect the Eskimos was also the company's Superintendent of Fisheries.

As for the Eskimos of the north and northwest coasts of Alaska, they went through a terrible time. The one good thing the Russians had done was to control liquor. When they left, whiskey and disease took over, and by 1884 the Eskimos of the north and northwest coasts were reduced from thousands to hundreds.

Probably disease did the most damage, but what the liquor did was more spectacular. Summer was the time of preparation for winter. It was the time to hunt and fill the meat pits. It had become, instead, the time to swap furs and ivory for whiskey. The Eskimos would go on a mighty celebration and wake up to find winter at hand and nothing in the meat pit. They would then starve to death. In 1888 an American revenue ship visited St. Lawrence Island at the southern end of Bering Strait. All the people of three neighboring villages—400 men, women, and children—were found to be dead from these causes.

Even for a sober man, meat was hard to come by now. In many areas the rifle had nearly wiped out the great beasts of the Far North. The walrus and the whale, the seal and the caribou, were all but gone. Dr. Sheldon Jackson, an American missionary who had been appointed Superintendent of Education, started to bring in tame reindeer to take the place of the vanished caribou. He began to change Eskimos from hunters to herdsmen. He began to bring them some education, some medical care, and some legal protection.

His task was like one of those impossible ones set for Hercules. Eskimos, he found, weren't easy to change, and the frontier whites put every obstacle in his path. Why help the dirty, wretched natives to survive? they asked. What good were they?

But the United States government had begun to feel its responsibility toward the Eskimos. In 1892 it brought in the first sizable herd of reindeer and hired Lapps from Norway to teach the Eskimos how to care for and breed the animals. And to everyone's amazement—except Dr. Jackson's—the experiment began to work.

Civilization without quotation marks had come to the Far North at last.

26. THE ACORN EATERS OF CALIFORNIA

When the Europeans found them, most of the California Indians lived very simply. In all the area of the United States none lived more so, except the people of the Great Basin—the Nevada-Utah deserts—next door east. Most had no farming and made only a little crude pottery. Most had no wealth of art except in basketry; no fancy dance costumes or carved and painted masks; no leagues and confederacies; even no formal governing councils.

And yet California was more thickly settled than any other section north of Mexico. A bewildering variety of people lived each in its own tiny country. Most of them believed they had always lived where they were and had sprung directly from the earth.

There was plenty of food easily got. Acorn flour, which the Indians made by pounding the acorns and leaching out the bitter tannic acid, was the staff of life. Fish and shellfish came next. Then came every kind of game, reptile, and bird. And finally various kinds of nuts, clovers, berries, grasses, cactus fruit, yucca, and sage.

Life was easy, and this made for leisure. Leisure and many people together are supposed to make for progress. But here century after century passed and things stayed the same. As in the case of the Eskimos, one has to look at the people a thousand years apart to see any change. They seem to have been content just to drift and dream on their sunny oceans of time. Maybe the principal occupation was being very merry.

Painted and feathered California Indians drawn in 1806 by a German artist. ROBERT B. HONEYMAN COLL., OAKLAND ART MUSEUM

The oldest inhabitants of California had probably been there a long time indeed. They may even have been descendants of the very earliest people to come into the New World. In the 1,000 years between 500 B.C. and A.D. 500, newcomers speaking various languages spread into California. By about A.D. 1200, a great many different peoples had become settled, each in its little homeland. Some of the northwest coast customs crept down into California. There, instead of the raven, the giant California condor was worshiped. From somewhere the Chumash seamen of that coast also learned to make plank boats by lashing planks together with sinew and calking them with asphalt. They are the only plank canoes known in the hemisphere, except for one spot on the coast of Chile.

North of San Francisco Bay, basket-making reached a very high point. Among the Pomos, the baskets dripped with feathers and beads, and some were so tightly woven that they could hold water. The skill of the Pomos was really unbelievable. Some baskets were woven just to exhibit craftsmanship. Baskets were made no bigger than a pinhead with stitches so tiny they cannot be seen with the naked eye.

Everywhere the ancient fears existed. People dared not speak the name of the dead. They were afraid of the shaman's magic power. And all feared the mysterious force that touched adolescent girls. An adolescent girl was dangerous. She had to hide her eyes so she would not wither trees or drive away the game.

Shamans held contests in which they tried to outwizard each other. From these contests, perhaps, came the group ceremonies that became sacred dances. They were repeated year after year. All winter long the dance cycles went on. They were inspired by the myths and the dreaming that sprang up on California soil—very little was borrowed from other places.

A Spanish expedition touched briefly on the upper California coast in 1602-03. But for the next 166 years the region was left more or less alone. Then in the spring of 1769, Spanish frontiersmen, priests, and soldiers pushed up overland with Indian allies to San Diego. Next year an expedition got to Monterey. During the next 50 years or so, 21 mission stations were planted. They started down at San Diego and finished up some 40 miles north of San Francisco.

The missions lived off Indian lands and by Indian labor. That was fair exchange, the priests thought, for teaching the natives the ways of Christianity and civilization. The "Mission Indians," of whom there grew to be more than 21,000, lived at the missions in large pueblos and worked at every trade from adobe-making to soap-making, from sheep-herding to pigeon tending. But the once merry and idle California Indians did not take to the new ways with enthusiasm. They had to be held by force and learned all about shackles, hobbles, stocks, imprisonment, and flogging. Some ran away. Some stubbornly died. There were a few armed revolts, but none of any consequence—these people were hopelessly simple when it came to war. In the main they just crumpled up. They collaped at the first toll of the mission bell.

Their very look changed. Two hundred years before, travelers who saw the California coast Indians described them as tall, frank, and handsome. But these Mission Indians were pictured as short, dark, and above all dirty and spiritless. The Fathers shook their heads over their charges. They were "lazy, stupid, jealous, gluttonous,

MUSEO NAVAL, MADRID

This drawing shows Christianized Indians at Carmel's mission lined up under the attentive eyes of Franciscan friars to welcome a visiting French scientific expedition.

timorous," they said. And certainly they acted as if they took no pleasure in living. "I have never seen any of them laugh," wrote a European artist who visited the San Francisco mission. "I have never seen a single one look anyone in the face. They have the air of taking no interest in anything."

But if the Indians stubbornly refused to prosper, the missions did. Thousands of horses and hundreds of thousands of cattle and sheep grazed on the millions of acres of mission lands. Crops of wheat, corn, and beans ran to 120,000 bushels a year. Mission storerooms were treasure houses of wine, leather, wool, oil, and other such riches. Who knows? Perhaps in time the missions might have transformed the spiritless Indians into solid colonial people. They did in other lands. But here time ran out. The missions were in business, on the average, only about half a century. Then Spain's New World colonies took fate into their own hands. They fought and won their independence. Mexico became an independent kingdom in 1821 and three years later was a republic.

California, for the time being, remained a possession of Mexico. But great changes took place. The wealthy missions were destroyed. The mission lands were supposed to go back to the Indians, but they didn't. They were carved up into the great California ranchos, and the Mission Indians were scattered like quail. The carving up was just being finished when the Mexican

War broke out. At the end of the war California belonged to the United States. Then gold was discovered, and in 1850 California became a full-fledged state.

A new chapter opened for the United States of America. For the California Indians it had already begun. They were killed off in what seems to have been the biggest single spree of massacring in American history. Before the gold rush of 1849 there were more than 100,000 Indians in California. Ten years later there were perhaps 30,000. By 1900 there were roughly half that. Eighty-five thousand California Indians disappeared in fifty years.

The frontier policy of clear out the Redskins came in with the stampede of treasure seekers. The white adventurers were trigger-happy, and the Indians were obliging—occasionally they killed or robbed miners or drove off livestock. This was reason enough for a "war." Whooping bands of the new California citizens formed companies of Indian fighters and butchered Indians right and left in a long series of Indian "wars." It was a quite profitable occupation—the fighters asked for and received pay and expenses from the government. As the gold diggings played out and times grew hard, fighting the Indians became a more and more attractive trade.

It was not good to be a California Indian in the 1850s. Especially if you were a woman. Or a child. In fifteen years some 3,000 to 4,000 Indian children were stolen to be sold as servants or laborers.

Men were enslaved in a different fashion. In Los Angeles the degraded ex-Mission Indians were arrested for drunkenness regularly every Saturday night. Sunday they spent in jail. And on Monday morning they were regularly bailed out for $2 or $3

COLLECTION OF CULL WHITE

These converts to Christianity were photographed with Father P. J. De Smet, a Northwest missionary, in 1860. Among the Indians there was more interest in education than Christianity. But when the Nez Perce asked for teachers, they got missionaries. Indeed, no other kind of white teacher was known to the Indians beyond the frontier.

a head by anyone who could use an Indian for a week's work.

The liquor sold to the Indians was real firewater, sometimes mixed with rot-gut acids. The result was that every week there were wild jamborees in which Indian men, women, and children brawled tooth and nail. "Those thousands of honest, useful people were absolutely destroyed in this way," wrote an indignant Los Angeles resident who saw it all.

When the Fifties were over, most of the survivors were put on ragged little reservations where they were expected to dwindle away in peace. They didn't quite, though many stocks became extinct. White men watched with a philosophic shrug. Didn't Indians *have* to give way? They were sacrifices, as a government inspector said, for the "great cause of civilization, which, in the natural course of things, must exterminate Indians."

It was the same frontier story that happened everywhere, but here it was speeded up so that the California people seem to have vanished in an instant. An aged Indian could quite possibly have seen the whole story in his own lifetime. He might have lived through everything from the coming of the Spanish colonizers to the extermination of the Fifties.

One island woman did even better. In her time she had seen the Russian and Aleut sea-otter hunters come to the Santa Barbara islands. Then groups from the missions had rounded up and taken away all those who could be caught. In 1835 Mexican officials had taken away the last of the natives still living on her island—it was San Nicolas, farthest offshore. The woman was left behind when she ran back from the boat to find her child, who had been overlooked. Nobody missed her. Anyway no boat came back. The child soon died, and the woman was left alone and forgotten on that island of winds and fogs for 18 years.

She had the houses of her people to live in, houses made of the ribs and jawbones of whales, with walls of skins. There were seals, birds, fish, shellfish, and roots for her to eat. And she dressed herself in warm gowns of birdskins.

She was found by accident and taken into Santa Barbara, which had become an American town. People tried to locate some of the Indians who had lived on the other offshore islands, and a number of them were brought to see her. But no one could understand her language. She died within a few months, although she was given the best of care.

27. BEULAH LAND

East of the Sierra Nevada lived the most deprived Indians in the entire United States area. Roaming in small bands without number, they picked up a scanty living from their deserts and barren mountains. They gathered wild seed and grasshoppers. They dug roots and hooked lizards out of their holes. Their houses were flimsy brush wickiups. They were too busy finding something to eat to build much—houses or anything else. Their ceremonies were just family affairs. There wasn't enough to eat in any one place for large gatherings.

All the Indians in the Great Basin proper spoke some Shoshonean tongue and had a Shoshonean look about them. They were short-legged and dark-skinned. Around the edges of the Great Basin other languages were spoken, but the people and their ways were not different from those in the Basin.

On the endless deserts of the mid-Basin the bands were desperately poor. Also they were very weak. So they made little trouble when miners and ranchers moved into their country. In the end the people usually attached themselves to ranches or towns. They worked now and then. Or they became beggars. But anyway they managed to stay on their native soil, where they had lived for many thousands of years. Whites called them Digger Indians—because they were forever digging up roots to eat—and thought them scarcely worth kicking out of the way.

To many of the ever-hungry mid-Basin people a horse was only something else to eat. But in the far western reaches, in the 1850s and 1860s, the Paiutes and others raided California ranchos to get horses to ride. These were the Indians who attacked the Pony Express riders and the stagecoaches that came intruding into their country. A number of tribes on the eastern and northern edges of the Basin had gotten the use of horses and had become rather splendid horse Indians. The Northern Shoshonis of the Rockies especially. One branch of these people, known as the Comanches, had become the finest horsemen and the toughest warriors in all America.

Westward of the mountain Shoshonis lived the Nez Perces, the Palouses, the Walla Wallas, and the Yakimas. All of them had been river people, fishing salmon for a living. They took to horses with joy. Hunting now became more important than fishing, and especially the yearly buffalo hunt. At the same time everything took on

At the time of the white man's arrival, many small Indian bands and tribes lived in the region beyond the Rockies. The ones who played important roles in the history of the area are indicated on the map at the right.

OKANAGAN
KUTENAI
BLOOD
MAKAH
COEUR D'ALENE
KALISPEL
PIEGAN
QUINAULT
COLVILLE
WASHINGTON
SKOKOMISH
SPOKAN
WENATCHEE
MISSOURI RIVER
N
PUYALLUP
NISQUALLY
FLATHEAD
PALOUSE
MONTANA
COWLITZ
YAKIMA
CHINOOK
WASCO
WALLA WALLA
KLICKITAT
NEZ PERCE
UMATILLA
COLUMBIA RIVER
TILLAMOOK
CAYUSE
SNAKE RIVER
YELLOWSTONE RIVER
KALAPOOIA
SIUSLAW
IDAHO
OREGON
BANNOCK
WYOMING
KLAMATH
MODOC
SHOSHONI
SHOSHONI
KAROK
YUROK
HUPA
SHASTA
PAIUTE
WINTU
WINTUN
GOSIUTE
GREAT SALT LAKE
UTE
MAIDU
PATWIN
SHOSHONI
SACRAMENTO RIVER
POMO
WASHO
NEVADA
UTAH
MIWOK
PAIUTE
COSTANOAN
MONO
COLORADO RIVER
YOKUTS
NAVAHO
PACIFIC OCEAN
PANAMINT
SALINAN
HOPI
HAVASUPAI
CALIFORNIA
WALAPAI
CHEMEHUEVI
CHUMASH
ARIZONA
MOHAVE
YAVAPAI
CAHUILLA
PIMA
SALT RIVER
SCALE
0 30 60 90 MILES
MARICOPA
GILA RIVER
YUMA
PAPAGO

the color of the Plains Indians. Houses became tipis. Full-dress fringed skins and feathered war bonnets came into fashion. And flowered bead designs blossomed on anything that would hold still to be stitched.

All these people were proud and warlike. Of them all the Nez Perces, who lived where Idaho, Oregon, and Washington come together, were the most powerful. Lewis and Clark guessed there were 6,000 of them. Like the Shoshonis, whose Sacagawea guided the explorers, the Nez Perces were friendly, hospitable, and helpful to them. And not only to them. They helped the other Americans who passed through their country during the next 50 years. The Americans often sorely tried their friendship. Yet through all those 50 years and more, not one American lost his life at Nez Perce hands.

Such were the Nez Perces and their neighbors, such as the Bannocks to their south and the Flatheads to their northeast. The Flathead, incidentally – whose real name was Salish—didn't flatten their heads but left them as nature made them. The name Flatheads was given them by people of the northwest coast who did deform their own skulls—into a point. By comparison the heads of the Salish seemed flat to them.

Most of these tribes were friendly to the first American settlers. And, as we said, the Nez Perces and Shoshonis were especially so. Washakie, a chief of the Wyoming Shoshonis, even received a memorial of thanks, signed by 9,000 emigrants. He had helped them to cross difficult fords and to get back stock that had strayed. More important, he had kept his people out of quarrels even when an unruly emigrant seemed bent on one.

But the first settlers to the Oregon country were not looking for trouble. They were looking for a Promised Land of corn and wine, green grass and fertile soil. Beulah Land they called it in their hymns, after the land of heavenly joy described by Pilgrim in *Pilgrim's Progress.* They met Indian friendship with friendship just as genuine.

The first real trouble came in 1847 when the Whitman mission among the Cayuse Indians was destroyed. The 12 Americans there, including Dr. Whitman and his wife, were killed. What the immediate cause of the massacre was isn't clear. It is said that the Cayuses were angry because more and

SMITHSONIAN INSTITUTION, BUREAU OF AMERICAN ETHNOLOGY

Washakie, illustrious war chief of the Eastern Band of the Wyoming Shoshoni, helped the first American settlers to such an extent—including fighting on their side when other western tribes caused trouble—that the whites presented him with a memorial of gratitude.

more white men were coming into their land. They feared their country would be taken from them and that the missionaries were in league with those who would do it. A measles epidemic just before the murders helped to heat things up, for a couple of hundred Cayuses had died in a few weeks. Wasn't it likely, thought the Indians, that the missionaries had let loose the sickness?

Settlers at once formed a volunteer army and took revenge. Then they asked Congress to send the military. To make peace, the Cayuses finally turned over five of the Whitman murderers. At any rate, five men were turned over who played the part for the sake of saving the rest of the people. They were duly tried and hanged.

In the early 1850s a new rush of people came into Oregon. Many of them were ex-gold-rushers, fresh from exterminating the Indians of California. This, and the availability of the United States Army, which had been on hand ever since the Cayuse War, started the frontier process going of its own accord. For the next ten years it rolled merrily along.

There were the usual councils, large and small, the usual treaty chiefs who had no authority to sign anything away, and the usual stubborn bands who didn't want to obey the treaty chiefs' treaties. Then came the usual force to make them. Some tribes, as usual, didn't want to make any land-ceding treaties at all. So as usual their country was overrun by border-jumpers. Then the usual incidents took place, followed by the usual wars.

As the Indians became more and more cowed, the whites became more and more lawless. That brought about new wars. Merchants who sold goods at high prices to volunteer Indian chasers were eager for hostilities, which meant profits. So they went all-out for bloodshed. "Let our motto be extermination, and death to all opposers," said a newspaper in Yreka, a trading town on the California-Oregon border. At the same time it must be said that a good many of the Oregon and Washington settlers were opposers. They had the courage to sympathize with the Indians when it was dangerous to do so. There were farmers who hid Indian friends in their houses when the troops or the volunteers were on the warpath. However, the anti-Indian people were stronger and generally got their way.

A great treaty-making council was held at Walla Walla in 1855 with the tribes of the Cascades. Kamaikan, a leader of the Yakimas, was dead set against confinement on reservations. He opposed the idea even when the United States commissioners offered to make him supreme chief of all the tribes gathered there. After long argument and much pressure, each of the 14 bands was allowed to select its own favorite home valley as a reservation, and on these terms the treaties were signed.

But three months afterward war broke out. Miners and settlers didn't even wait for Congress to ratify the treaties. A gold strike had been made, and the white men streamed into the treaty lands. The Yakimas attacked the white squatters and killed an Indian agent. Governor Stevens called out the troops. And a violent war was on. It spread far and lasted three years. It ended with two or three dozen Indian leaders being hanged. Kamaikan, wounded, escaped to Canada.

Wars continued. Raids and counter-raids continued. But for most of the tribes of the Northwest there remained only the last scene to play. The curtain was about to come down.

28. CHIEF JOSEPH OF THE NEZ PERCE

SMITHSONIAN INSTITUTION, BUREAU OF AMERICAN ETHNOLOGY

Chief Joseph was brave, humane, and a great statesman of his people.

Among the Nez Perces there lived a man of importance named Joseph. It was a name given to him by Reverend Spalding, whose school Joseph had attended.

He was the son of a Cayuse father, but his wife was a Nez Perce, and Joseph had been at the great Walla Walla council of 1855 as one of the Nez Perce spokesmen. The treaty he signed there reserved for his Nez Perce band what it claimed as its ancient home. This was the Wallowa Valley along the Snake River near the mouth of the Grande Ronde, where the states of Oregon, Washington, and Idaho meet.

After 1855 the Nez Perces, true to their long friendship for the United States, stuck to peace while all Oregon was on fire with war. In 1858 they rescued a body of American troops. And when the Civil War broke out and the United States government had its hands full, the Nez Perces refused to join any trouble-making plots.

In 1863 a new treaty was made. It ceded the Wallowa Valley to the government for settlement. Joseph's band had not taken part in these negotiations and Joseph protested. The other Nez Perces had acted without authority in ceding this land, he said, and the new treaty violated the treaty of 1855. He and his band stayed on in the valley although white settlers started moving in and the usual incidents happened.

In 1871 Joseph died. The leadership of his band now went to a son named Hin-mah-too-yah-laht-ket (Thunder Rolling in the Mountains). To the Americans he was known as Young Joseph, and later as Chief Joseph.

The Nez Perces are so often described as noble, handsome, brave, true-hearted and, in general, excellent in all respects that it seems likely they may have been so. When it comes to Young Joseph, the descriptions reach the heights. He was, so they say, boundlessly wise, eloquent, good, and merciful. In his pictures as a young man he is clearly no mountain Indian. He is a hero straight out of a romance by Sir Walter Scott.

In the spring of 1876 a settler killed a man of Young Joseph's band. It was one more of those hostile incidents which the Nez Perces had so far endured without striking back. Young Joseph did not strike back even now. "As to the murderer," he said, "I have made up my mind. I have come to the conclusion to let him escape and enjoy health and not take his life for the one he took. I am speaking as though I spoke to the man himself. I pronounce the sentence that he shall live."

Young Joseph and his people didn't want to leave their valley. It was their home. Also, they were horsemen. Their wealth was in their thousands of horses, many of them the blue Appaloosas with five-finger-

WASHINGTON STATE HISTORICAL SOCIETY

Old Joseph, father of the famous Chief Joseph who led the Nez Perce retreat.

spotted rumps which had become famous as the Nez Perce war and hunting horses. If they moved to a reservation, each head of a family would have only 20 acres. This was far from enough for a stockman. But to avoid a hopeless clash with the authorities, Young Joseph at last agreed to take his people out of the valley. They would settle on the Lapwai Reservation where the government wanted them to go.

While the Nez Perces were getting ready to move, an unfortunate thing happened. White neighbors of theirs took the opportunity to steal several hundred of their horses. The departing people were already heartsick, homesick, and angry. Now they counted up their wrongs. At last a moment came when Young Joseph could no longer restrain his young men. In a night and a day a few of them took vengeance and murdered 18 settlers. Then out came the troops. After 72 years of peace, the Nez Perces were at war. Joseph had said, "Rather than have war I would give up my country. I would give up everything." Now he had

GILCREASE INSTITUTE, TULSA, OKLAHOMA

Chief Joseph approaching to deliver his famous speech of surrender to American officers.

no choice.

He decided to lead his band—400 to 500 people — to safety in Canada. For four months he fought his way through and around Army units that were rushed in from all sides to head him off. With his 100 to 200 warriors Joseph fought a campaign over 1,000 mountain miles. He was burdened with all his refugee people and their belongings. Yet General Howard, the Army Commander, was not able to gain an advantage though he had more men, more guns, and was unburdened. Time and again the Americans suffered heavy losses. And at last it began to appear that Chief Joseph was a military genius.

He fought more than a dozen battles with four different Army columns. In a daring night raid he would carry off the enemy's horses so they couldn't pursue him. Or he made a clever feint that turned the pursuing columns around to run into each other. Or he simply fought and out-fought the enemy with his handful of dazzling cavalrymen. Several times the Nez Perces suffered casualties. In one engagement 89 were killed, 50 of them being women and children. But they continued to march, and they continued to fight.

The war which the Nez Perces fought was one of the most extraordinary wars of which there is any record. For one thing, Chief Joseph allowed no scalping and there was none. Captive women were let go free. Peaceful families were not murdered. As for the courage and skill of the Nez Perces, they won the admiration of the enemy. General Miles, who finally cut off Joseph's retreat, had only praise for the Nez Perces. "In this skillful campaign," he said, "they have spared hundreds of lives and thousands of dollars' worth of property that they might have destroyed." In his opinion, Joseph's Nez Perces had "been grossly wronged in years past."

Joseph led his band—men, women, and children, wounded, maimed, and blind—through the Bitterroot Mountains, twice across the Rocky Mountains, through Yellowstone National Park, and across the Missouri River, to the Bear Paw Mountains. There, on Eagle Creek, within 30 miles of the Canadian border, he was stopped.

Chief Joseph knew that his retreat was cut off. But for two days he refused to give up. Then on the evening of a wintry day, just as the sun was setting, he surrendered. His people came pouring out of the burrows they had made in the hills, where they had been living without fires, eating the flesh of the dead horses. And now it could be seen how few of them were able-bodied warriors. Most of the people were aged, broken-down men and women, blind people, children, babies, and the wounded.

In the final attack, Joseph's little girl, about eight or nine years old, whom he was very fond of, fled in terror out on the prairie. It was supposed at the time that she had perished from cold and starvation. And this, too, was on Joseph's mind as he made his way to the enemy camp.

Lieutenant Wood, who was aide-de-camp to General Howard and was present at the surrender, later wrote down everything exactly as it happened. Here is how he describes the scene:

"Joseph came up to the crest of the hill, upon which stood Gen. Howard, Gen. Miles, an interpreter, and myself. Joseph was the only one mounted, but five of his principal men clung about his knees and pressed close to the horse, looking up at him, and talking earnestly in low tones. Joseph rode with bowed head, listening attentively, apparently, but with perfectly immobile face. As he approached the spot where we were standing, he said something, and the five men who were with him halted. Joseph rode forward alone, leaped from his horse, and, leaving it standing, strode toward us. He opened the blanket which was wrapped around him, and handed his rifle to Gen. Howard, who motioned him to deliver it to Gen. Miles, which Joseph did. Standing back, he folded his blanket again across his chest, leaving one arm free, somewhat in the manner of a Roman senator with his toga, and, half turning toward the interpreter, said:

" 'Tell General Howard I know his heart. What he told me before, in Idaho, I have it in my heart. I am tired of fighting . . . My people ask me for food, and I have none to give. It is cold, and we have no blankets, no wood. My people are starving to death. Where is my little daughter? I do not know. Perhaps, even now, she is freezing to death. Hear me, my chiefs. I have fought; but from where the sun now stands, Joseph will fight no more forever.'

"And he drew his blanket across his face, after the fashion of Indians when mourning or humiliated, and instead of walking towards his own camp, walked directly into ours, as a prisoner."

Joseph asked that he and his people should be allowed to go back to the reservation which had been provided for them in the first place. This was promised him. But the promise was broken by the government, and they were sent to Indian Territory. There in the malarial bottoms all of his own six children and most of his band died. After long delay, in 1885 he was allowed to go with the last of his people to northern Washington.

"No supplies were provided for them," Lieutenant Wood tells us. "They marched from Indian Territory to their new home, and arrived on the edge of winter in a destitute condition, experiencing great suffering."

And he adds something that weighs on the heart:

"I think that, in his long career, Joseph cannot accuse the Government of the United States of one single act of justice."

29. THE PEOPLE OF DREAMS

When in 1519 Cortes landed his ten stallions, five mares and a foal in horseless America, he had no idea the animals were coming home. But in a sense they were. For the prehistoric horse was born in the Americas many millions of years ago. Here took place all its development from a creature no bigger than a fox. At the close of the Ice Age, for reasons unknown, the horse became extinct in the New World. However, horses had long before that time spread to the Old World, doubtless across a Siberian land bridge. And now, having traveled all the way around the earth, they had come back to the place of their birth.

Perhaps they knew it. In any case, they went forth and multiplied at an astonishing rate. Horses were brought into Peru in 1532. Three years later they had entered the horse heaven that is Argentina. By 1600 they were streaming over the Argentine pampas in herds too vast to count. The people there, and in the scrub-covered country on the north known as the Chaco, took to horses with passion, and they utterly changed the ways of their world.

In North America, Santa Fe was the early horse center. The Spanish officials knew what an advantage the animals gave them and tried hard to keep the Indians from learning how to manage horses. But who was going to do the herding if not the Indians? Naturally they learned. And having learned, they stole horses by the bunch, by the herd, by the multitude, from the huge ranches of Chihuahua and New Mexico.

A Blackfoot medicine-pipe carrier wearing the distinctive coiled hairdo of his station.

After the Pueblo revolt that drove the Spaniards out of Santa Fe, the horse frontier moved much faster than the white frontier. Horses fanned out over the West. And their hoofbeats were like a flourish of drums announcing a marvelous new life.

The deserts of Utah and Nevada were too poor in grazing and water for a man to keep a horse. But the Ute people of the western slopes of the Rockies took to horses—and they passed from tribe to tribe. By the 1690s the northern Shoshonis of Wyoming were learning the mysteries of managing the wonderful new animals. And now, with war feathers tied to their flying tails and with Shoshoni bowmen on their backs, horses trotted eastward to sweep across the endless plains. They sped in pursuit of the antelope, the buffalo, and the constant Shoshoni foes—the bold-hearted people of the northern plains known as the Blackfeet.

Brave they were. But any people on foot would be thrown into a panic by enemies transformed into centaurs nine feet tall that swooped on them like the whistling wind. The Blackfeet called on the Crees and Assiniboins for help. They came—and defeated a Shoshoni war party with the aid of another fantastic new weapon, the gun.

The horse frontier, moving in from the south and west, and the gun frontier, moving in from the east, met on the Great Plains. Out of that spectacular clash was born the figure of the American Indian that has displaced all others—the feather-streaming, buffalo-chasing, wild-riding, recklessly fighting Indian of the plains.

This Indian, shaped by the horse and the gun, came very late. He reached full glory only when the real Indian world was all but a memory. He was less sheer Indian than almost any who came before him, from the proto-Olmecs and the Mayas to the Creeks and Iroquois. And yet it is the image of this Indian that comes to mind when we think of Indians. It is the Plains Indian, decorated from war-bonnet band to moccasins with the white man's beads, that appears before us when we say the words "American Indian."

These modern Plains Indians had many roots. They sprang from farmers and hunters who had lived on the plains and their margins for untold centuries and from various tribes and nations that poured into the plains with the coming of the horse and gun.

The Blackfeet—whose name may refer to black-dyed moccasins—are thought to be the ancients of the northern plains, though how long they may have lived there none can guess. There were three tribes of them —the Blackfeet proper, the Bloods, and the Piegans. On the eve of the coming of the horse, they lived throughout Montana and far up into Alberta to the edge of the black northern forest.

East of the Piegans lived the Atsinas, brothers of the Arapahoes of the Wyoming plains. The country of the Yellowstone and its branches, the Powder and Big Horn rivers, belonged to the Absaroke, meaning the Crow-people, or Bird-people. They had once been part of the farming Hidatsa but had moved west and become hunters living in skin tipis. To the white men they were known as Crows.

In the northeast plains lived a part of Canada's Cree people, who had pressed down with the Hudson's Bay Company guns looking for beaver, and had become the Plains Crees. They drew their friends the Assiniboins after them from southern Ontario. A sizeable tribe these were. Not long before, they had separated from the Dakotas, the great Siouan-speaking nation.

The Ojibwas, because they were armed with trade guns, had driven the rest of the Dakotas and the Algonquian-speaking Cheyennes out of the forests of Wisconsin and eastern Minnesota. These two displaced nations, farmers as well as hunters, had a high order of courage, character, brains, and ability.

The Cheyennes crossed the wide Missouri and in the space of 50 years or so transformed themselves into horsemen. They became constant hunters and magnificent warriors.

The Dakotas, whose name means "allies," formed a true confederacy of seven tribes. Some of these tribes remained on the edge of the eastern forests and the high-grass prairie adjoining and kept on farming. Others, such as the tribe known as the Tetons, moved into the plains. Like the Cheyennes, they became Plains Indians of the first class. They were known the world over as such—the famous Sioux, a name coined by the French from an Algonquian term that means "enemies." There were many other Siouan peoples, but the Dakotas have usually been known as the Sioux, just as the Five Nations Iroquois were known as the Iroquois.

For all these people of the plains, newcomers and old residents alike, the horse

GLENBOW FOUNDATION, CALGARY

A woman of the Blood tribe rides on the broad Canadian plains.

brought a wonderful new life. Everything was easier with the horse, everything was better. Tipis could be larger, the number of possessions greater. Buffalo could be found miles away. They could be surrounded at a gallop and chased down if they stampeded. Dried meat and pemmican could be kept and moved by the ton. There was a wealth of new clothes, as well as spare time, and there were new delights.

Better still, there was time for war. And what is more, horses gave it an exciting new purpose. A man's fortune was counted in horses, a young man's future depended on horses. So horses became the object of war, and the capture of horses the main activity in war. The rest of what made up war—the fighting and the danger of death—became bound around with endless ceremony. There were warrior societies, each with its special costumes, special grades, special manners, special rites, and special taboos.

War called for fancy tricks, fancy riding, fancy fighting. Two of the three great feats of war were to capture by stealth an enemy's best horses—the valued stallion or the fleet hunters he kept close beside his lodge—and to touch the enemy's body in battle. This last was called "counting coup" and involved a complicated system of war honors. The taking of scalps was not important—only the Crees and Teton Dakotas looked upon a scalp as a first-class trophy. The Dakotas, if they had time, would take all the skin of the head and face. But before the coming of the Europeans there was not much scalping. It was the scalp bounties that helped to spread scalping throughout the Indian world.

Above all, the new world of the horse brought time and temptation to dream. The plains had always been a place for dreams, but with horses they were more so. Something happens to a man when he gets on a horse, in a country where he can ride at a run forever. It is quite easy for him to

C. R. SMITH COLLECTIO

Plains life had a savage beauty. In his painting of a buffalo chase, Montana's cowboy artist Charles Russell captured the rhythm that made horse and rider one. The Indian's pony carried its rider without guidance, leaving the hunter's hands free to shoot.

think he is living in a myth. He feels either like a god or feels closer to God. There seems never to have been a race of plains horsemen that was not either extremely proud or extremely religious.

A man dreamed of the horse he would capture, and of what sort of feathers to wear in his hair, and the paint to put on his face, and the foe he would kill, and the girls he would marry, and the pattern to put on his shield, and the way he would die.

The principal way to get a vision was by means of the Sun Dance, a rite practiced by nearly all the people of the plains. For days and nights (usually four) those who would take part in this dance, which was scarcely a dance, went without food or water. They stared fixedly at the top of a central pole, where a red-painted buffalo skull or some other object represented the sun. The "dancers" stood more or less in one place, rising up and down on their toes or shuffling a little backward and forward. They held eaglebone whistles in their mouths to sound with each breath. For those who lasted long enough, a vision might be granted. Some, to fulfill a vow or to wring pity from the gods, tortured themselves. They would run skewers through the muscles in their chests or backs and swing from thongs until the skewers were torn loose.

The Creator, the Old Person, God by whatever name, spoke through dreams and visions over much of the Indian world. But the plains people went to extremes in this conversation. They were extreme in all their emotions. Death was a matter for magnificent emotion. Mourning brought wild displays of grief.

The third great feat of war was bravery in rescuing a dead body from the enemy so it could not be mutilated. A man risked his life for that.

GILCREASE INSTITUTE, TULSA, OKLAHOMA

George Catlin's painting of an eastern plains warrior roping a wild pony.

30. WAR ON THE PLAINS

French fur traders were in the plains long before Americans got there. The French had a knack for getting along with Indians. So, in the main, did the American mountain men, the "free" trappers, who followed the French into the plains. Only one nation was unfailingly the mountain man's enemy—the Blackfoot confederacy. And this was because among the Canadian fur companies that traded on the Saskatchewan, it was considered part of good business to urge Indians to kill off the competition. The Blackfeet simply followed instructions and killed off any American trappers who came their way.

Things moved fast in the plains—by the 1840s the mountain men had vanished from the trapped-out beaver streams. Their place, in the plains and the Rockies, was being taken by wagon trains of emigrants bound for the West Coast. The frontier stole in from the east like dusk, and at once the Indians felt its touch in the form of whiskey, disease, and an increase in war.

The Southern Cheyennes and Arapahoes fought the Comanches and Kiowas. The Sioux and the Northern Cheyennes fought the Crows. Most of the people of the farther plains were hostile to the Shoshonis, who ranged down from the mountains, and to the Pawnees, who ranged westward from the eastern plains. The eastern Indians who had been driven across the Mississippi were fearful adversaries, for they were expert with guns when the plains people as yet had few of them.

All this Indian-versus-Indian fighting interfered with the trade and travel of Americans. Excitable war parties were everywhere. They menaced and frightened emigrants and sometimes stole their stock. American troops were marched up and down the plains several times in the 1830s and 1840s, to the delight of the Indians, who admired the show of color and guns and, most of all, the soldiers' swords. "Big Knives" came to be the polite name for white Americans among the plains people —as it was among most other Indians throughout the United States. In 1849 two military posts were established along the Platte. And in 1851 the great mountain man Tom Fitzpatrick, who had been appointed United States Indian Agent, held a great council near one of them—Fort Laramie.

The place was Horse Creek. Here gathered the greatest assembly of Indians in Plains history. Some 8,000 to 12,000 people were present — Assiniboins, Atsinas, Arikaras, Crows, Shoshonis, Sioux, Cheyennes, and Arapahoes. Some of these nations never remembered having met before except in battle.

All agreed on a general peace and promised to be more considerate of emigrants. The United States, on its side, promised to keep troops in the plains to protect the Indians from plunder by whites.

Three years later, not more than 10 miles from the scene of this great peace council, the wars of the United States

WOLF ROBE, CHEYENNE

against the Plains Indians were opened.

The immediate cause was a bedraggled emigrant cow (said to have been abandoned), killed by a Minneconjou Sioux for its hide. The emigrant put in a claim at Fort Laramie for damages. Spokesmen from the Sioux camp offered $10. The emigrant demanded $25. The Sioux couldn't meet the price. A young lieutenant who fancied himself a fire-eater took 32 men and two cannon and went to the Sioux camp to drag out the cow killer. There were many lodges of Oglala and Brule people, and among the Brules a few lodges of Minneconjous, all of them subtribes of the Teton Dakotas. An argument started, and the lieutenant had the Brule chief shot down on the spot. In the fight that followed, the lieutenant and all his men were killed.

This was not the first blood spilled between the plains people and the soldiers who had come to protect them. The summer before, some Laramie troops had killed three or four Sioux in a misunderstanding. The Sioux had recognized it as such. But this was the first blood of American soldiers.

The American public clamored for revenge. They got it the following summer when an army of 1,300 men marched into the plains and destroyed a Brule village near the forks of the Platte, killing 86 persons. At a conference in the spring of 1856, the Brules promised to turn over the man who killed the cow.

That same spring an argument arose with a band of Cheyennes over a stray horse. It led to an attack by the military on a Cheyenne family that had nothing to do with the matter. Other Cheyennes then killed a trapper who had nothing to do with the military attack. Troops then attacked a group of unsuspecting Cheyennes who had had nothing to do with any of the above, killing a half dozen of them and seizing all their horses and property. Cheyennes then plundered two wagon trains, killing seven innocent persons, including a woman and two children.

Things dragged along like this until the summer of 1857. Then Colonel E. V. Sumner set out with a strong force to put a stop to it. On a July day he met the flower of the southern Cheyennes in the plains along the Solomon River in what is now Kansas. It was one of the few real picture-book battle scenes in all Indian history. Some 300 mounted warriors, drawn up in battle line, were singing their war song. All were in full war costume. In the pre-battle ceremonies, their great medicine man, Ice, had told them he had been granted power to render the soldiers' bullets harmless, and Ice himself had picked the battleground. So the Cheyennes were confident of victory. But Colonel Sumner's soldiers did not fire guns—at his command the cavalry charged with drawn sabers.

No medicine had been made against sabers. The Cheyennes shot a panicky flight of arrows and fled. A peace was made the following spring.

But war had settled down to stay. Peace, from now on, would be like sunny days in winter. Everyone believed, or said he did, that each peace treaty would last forever. But in the spring hostility would suddenly break out again. And as the frontier reached out to take in the plains, the times of peace grew briefer and more clouded and the times of war longer and more violent.

In 1858 gold was found in Cherry Creek at the foot of the Rockies near present-day Denver, Colorado. The Pike's Peak gold

RAIN IN THE FACE, SIOUX

SMITHSONIAN INSTITUTION, BUREAU OF AMERICAN ETHNOLOGY

Little Crow, leader of the Sioux uprising, was shot by a farmer.

rush got under way the following summer. In the next three years 80,000 people poured into the plains. More gold strikes and then fabulous silver strikes followed. Real-estate promoters appeared and settlers followed the miners. In less than ten years railroads were being driven across the buffalo plains.

The frontier wrapped its coils around the Indians of the plains and in due time swallowed them up. It was the same old story—treaties, disagreements within the Indian nations, new treaties wrenched from the Indians by force, quarrels, wars, a call for extermination, and the bloody, long-drawn-out ending.

What was it all for? General George Crook, who fought the Indians and fought them hard, put it into a sentence: "Greed and avarice on the part of the whites—in other words, the almighty dollar is at the bottom of nine-tenths of all our Indian troubles."

Like so many other Indian wars, the wars of the plains were dismal, dirty, and needless. But in our folklore they have become something like poetry. They are all the Indian wars rolled into one gaudy package, just as the Plains Indians are all the Indians rolled into one colorful figure.

SHARP NOSE. ARAPAHO

U.S. SIGNAL CORPS, NATIONAL ARCHIVES

SIGMUND SAMUEL CANADIANA GALLERY, ROYAL ONTARIO MUSE

Blackfoot tipis, decorated with figures symbolic of their owners' magic powers. War was the business of this tribe of the high plains. They were unfailingly hostile to American trappers.

A thousand stories tell us that never were there such brave knights, such reckless horsemanship, such noble heroes as on the plains. Above all, never was there such rainbow color brought to battle—the painted shields and war horses, the painted eyes and bodies, the buffalo hats, the lynx-skin headdresses with an eagle feather for each slain foe, the rippling war bonnets, the jewel-work of beads and porcupine quills.

The reality was very different.

The Minnesota Sioux, the four Dakota subtribes known as the Santees, had signed a treaty in 1851. They felt cheated by it and were cheated also in their reservation life. In the summer of 1862 the Santees tried to kill all the whites in their country, under the leadership of one of their chiefs, 60-year-old Little Crow. They murdered some 700 settlers and killed 100 soldiers before they were driven out of Minnesota to join the other Dakotas on the plains. Several dozen Santee chiefs and warriors were hanged. Little Crow, a fugitive, was shot by a farm youth while foraging for berries.

For the southern Cheyennes and Arapahoes things had been very pleasant through the early days of Denver. Then in 1861 a treaty was made which only a few men could be induced to sign. Some said afterward they didn't know what they were signing. The treaty ceded most of southern Cheyenne and Arapaho territory. Worse, it contained a clause that government officials later said permitted a railroad to go through what Indian lands were left. A railroad meant white settlements, and this meant an end of the last of their country. When the Cheyenne and Arapaho people understood this, they threatened the treaty chiefs with death and forced them to cancel the treaty.

But peace held up until the spring of 1864. Then the Reverend J. M. Chivington, colonel of Colorado volunteers, reported that Cheyennes had stolen some cattle from a government contractor's herd. Quite likely it was not true—the Indians were blamed any time a white man lost a stray animal. But Colonel Chivington acted at once. His troops attacked families of unsuspecting Cheyennes, the Cheyennes attacked families of unsuspecting settlers, and another war was on.

The governor of Colorado got some of the alarmed Cheyennes to come to Denver for peace talks. The peace party was headed by Chief Black Kettle and the distinguished war chief White Antelope. They talked to the governor and, on the advice of the military commandant of Fort Lyon, set up their village on Sand Creek, 30 miles from the fort. The village was then destroyed in a stealthy sudden attack. Before the attack, Colonel Chivington said to his troops, mainly volunteers: "Kill and scalp all big and little; nits make lice." The boys, as he called the soldiers in his reports, did so with enthusiasm.

Black Kettle ran up both an American flag and a white flag, but the boys were having too much fun. They butchered any Indian in sight. Black Kettle's wife was shot down and passing soldiers fired seven more bullets into her body. Black Kettle managed to escape. White Antelope refused to run. He stood in front of his lodge and folded his arms and sang his death song. It was a good song and has been remembered: "Nothing lives long, except the earth and the mountains." He sang until he was cut down by bullets and died. He was some years past 70 at the time.

About 200 Cheyenne women and children were killed at Sand Creek and some 70 men and 40 or more Arapaho people who were with the Cheyennes. The boys went back to Denver and exhibited scalps and arms and legs in a theater. The boys had reason to be proud! This was probably the greatest victory—measured by the number of Indians killed—that the whites were to have in the Indian wars of the plains.

Not all Americans were proud of the boys. One, named Kit Carson, spoke of them as cowards and dogs. Nor did the settlers rejoice. The Cheyenne plains went up in flames during the next three years. In two summer months alone, 117 settlers were killed and their women and children dragged away as captives. Four years after Chivington's victory, a government commission said that there was scarcely anything in Indian history to equal the barbarity at Sand Creek.

U.S. SIGNAL CORPS, NATIONAL ARCHIVES

YOUNG MAN AFRAID OF HIS HORSES, SIOUX

CROW KING, SIOUX

U.S. SIGNAL CORPS, NATIONAL ARCHIVES

U.S. SIGNAL CORPS, NATIONAL ARCHIVES

SHORT BULL, SIOUX

LOW DOG, SIOUX

U.S. SIGNAL CORPS, NATIONAL ARCHIVES

31. CRAZY HORSE AND SITTING BULL

In a guerrilla war, invading troops are at a disadvantage. They can't lay hands on the guerrillas. So they punish other people. The easiest thing is to execute everybody in the nearest village.

After Sand Creek, Black Kettle made constant efforts for peace, believing that there was no other way for his people to stay alive. In the winter of 1868 his village, then camped on the Washita River in Oklahoma, was again attacked by troops. They were under orders to destroy a village and hang all the men and take all the women and children prisoner. This time Black Kettle was killed too. But men from nearby Arapaho, Kiowa, and Comanche villages came to the rescue, and the American commander withdrew. He left behind 19 of his men who had gone prisoner-catching, and all 19 were slain. The American commander was Lieutenant Colonel George A. Custer, and this was his first major engagement with Indians. It might be called Custer's first stand.

In 1874 gold was discovered in the Black Hills. After that the Indian wars reached their climax.

The Black Hills had been guaranteed to the Sioux by the treaty of 1868, which said that the Powder River country, including the Black Hills, was to be theirs forever and that no white men should ever be permitted to pass over this land or settle

U.S. SIGNAL CORPS, NATIONAL ARCHIVES

Sitting Bull, Sioux chief

on it. But when the news of the gold strike in the Black Hills spread, prospectors stole in, a few at first, then more and more. The Sioux protested. The Army stepped in then. It seized the miners and turned them over to a court. But as not one was found guilty, they all came right back and brought more prospectors with them.

Again the Sioux protested. And now the Government offered to buy the mining rights. It would pay $6,000,000 for them.

The Sioux laughed at the offer. More than that had already been taken out of their Black Hills, they said. If the Great Father wanted to buy their land and get rich, they wanted to get rich too. They would not sell for less than $50,000,000.

The Government saw that other means

of persuasion would have to be found. And now an order went out. The Sioux must come in and be "enrolled."

Most of the bands obeyed. But Crazy Horse of the Oglala, a warrior famed for his recklessness, would not come in. Neither would Tatanka Yotanka, Sitting Buffalo, known to the Americans as Sitting Bull. He was chief of the Hunkpapa division of the Teton Dakotas and one of the most able, honest, and idealistic statesmen in Indian history. Sitting Bull understood very well what was behind the order and sent back word: "I have no land to sell. We do not want any white men here."

A second order went out. If Sitting Bull did not come in, the Army would take drastic action against him.

"You can find me easily," Sitting Bull returned. "I will not run away."

So persuasion by means of the gun began. It was a difficult job, requiring many columns of troops and many scouts—Pawnees and Crows and Shoshonis who had joined the white soldiers to fight their old enemies of the plains.

In June 1876, General George Crook found the main body of unpersuaded Sioux in the valley of Rosebud Creek in southern Montana. The General, who was leading 1,000 or so soldiers, was attacked by a more or less equal number of warriors. But the ground kept growing Indians. Crook could not hold his own against them and limped back to his base of supplies to wait for more troops.

The Indians moved across the ridge to the next river west, the Little Big Horn. There they set up a large camp made up of Crazy Horse's people and Sitting Bull's people and allies from the other Sioux divisions and the Cheyennes.

Eight days after the battle with Crook, this camp was attacked on a Sunday afternoon by a regiment of cavalry. The attack was defeated. Crazy Horse, shouting, "Today is a good day to fight, today is a good day to die," led a rush that cut off half the attacking forces. Every man in this surrounded group of cavalrymen was killed in a desperate, blazing fight that lasted less than half an hour.

The attacking force had been the elite Seventh Cavalry, which had destroyed Black Kettle's camp on the Washita. The force had been led by Lieutenant Colonel Custer, who died in the battle along with more than 260 of his men.

The news reached the people on July 5, 1876. It caught the nation smack in the very middle of a great centennial celebration. That kind of humiliating defeat simply could not be handed to a modern nation of 40,000,000 people by a few scarecrow savages. Especially when it was in the act of congratulating itself on its first hundred years.

So the defeat was, in effect, the end of the wars of the plains. Crazy Horse and Sitting Bull had lost by winning. For now troops harried them without mercy, and the Indians had no means of keeping a standing army in the field indefinitely. They were separated into small bands and were hunted down or driven into Canada. After terrible suffering, Crazy Horse and his band laid down their arms. The Chief had been promised that not a hair of his head would be touched, but this promise was broken, and Crazy Horse was killed while trying to escape arrest.

"They say we massacred Custer," he declared. "But he would have done the same to us. We wanted to escape, but we were so hemmed in we had to fight."

The ending went on and on, like the

dying wail of a death song. It went on for years, while all the romance evaporated and the warriors of the plains were seen to be not knights such as never were but only bedraggled, scurrying creatures, hunted like fugitive convicts. So they were turned over to jailers who knew how to handle tough prisoners. And the greatest of warriors is no better than any weakling when he has nothing to do but crouch under guard and watch his people starve.

Well, it all ended. Through the years it wavered away and ended. The New York *Herald* was still calling for extermination in 1879, saying, "The continent is getting too crowded." But no one really took calls for extermination by gun seriously any more. Starvation, disease, and tough prison wardens were just as good anyway.

At the very end a religious craze seized the Indians. The religion was brought to them by a Nevada Paiute named Wovoka. The whites called it the Ghost Dance because it preached that the ghosts of dead Indians were on hand to help the living Indians in their hour of despair. A great revival spread among the emotional people of the plains, and the authorities were afraid the excitement might lead to riot and violence. Sitting Bull was killed then while being placed under arrest.

Three days after Christmas in 1890, a unit of the Seventh Cavalry arrested a band of some 300 Hunkpapa Sioux who were thought to be dangerous. Two-thirds of them were women and children. The Indians were held overnight and forced to camp in the center of a ring of 500 cavalrymen. Four Hotchkiss guns were set up and carefully sighted in on the Sioux camp. In the morning the troops formed a hollow square with the Indian camp in the middle. Then they disarmed the Sioux men, who were called out from the others to form a line. Somehow a disturbance began. It is said that someone fired a shot. In any case, the troops quite suddenly opened heavy fire into the Sioux camp. The Sioux men seem to have been shot down first and most of them were finished off at once, or in a few minutes. But enough people attacked the soldiers with their bare hands, or what weapons they still had, to kill 29 soldiers. The shooting went on as long as anyone, woman or child, remained to be shot at. Some of the women were pursued as far as three miles over the plains before they were caught and killed. A few are said to have escaped.

There has been dispute about the total number of Sioux dead. The military said there were no fewer than 200. But it was at least the second greatest victory for American arms in the wars of the plains.

The event took place on Wounded Knee Creek in South Dakota. The frozen dead were gathered up in wagons and buried together in a communal pit.

32. TROUBLE IN TEXAS

Apache comes from a Zuni word meaning enemy. It seems that it was first given as a name to the invaders who took over the lands of an abandoned pueblo called Navahu. These invaders were called the Apaches de Navahu. Or at least it sounded like that to the early Spaniards. Later on the name Apache spread to other related peoples all over the Southwest. The Apaches de Navahu, however, came to be known as the Navahos or, as the Spanish spelled it, *Navajo*. In time they were not included among the Apaches in general. The Navahos became a distinct tribe, gathering in new peoples and new customs until their ways, race, and language were considerably changed.

In the beginning all these—Apaches and Navahos — were Athapascan-speaking people. So they must have drifted down from the far northwest of Canada. This may have taken place 1,000 to 700 years ago. By the time the Americans began to come into the Southwest, most of these people had been living in their desert and mountain homes a long time and were as familiar with each rock and beast and useful plant as if they had been there forever. The Apaches

Frederic Remington's painting shows Indians dashing through gunfire to swoop up a fallen brave.

GILCREASE INSTITUTE, TULSA, OKLAHOMA

moved about quite a bit. But roughly they formed a ring around the country of the upper Rio Grande that was the center of the Pueblo world and of the early Spanish settlements. There were some three dozen separate bands of Apaches—excluding, of course, the Navahos—and they numbered perhaps somewhere between 5,000 and 6,000 people.

The Apaches centering in Arizona were all more or less alike. They got perhaps a fourth or a fifth of their food from farming and the rest from hunting and wild foods. Mescal (agave) and acorns came first among these wild foods. Then followed almost countless others, led by pinon, prickly pear, yucca, sunflower, mesquite, and saguaro. The Apaches east of the Rio Grande depended more on the buffalo.

For centuries while they were slowly moving south, the Apaches and Navahos were among the most important people of the Great Plains. But by the 1700s new people were invading from the north. These were the Comanches and Kiowas. Nearly all the Apaches of the plains got out of their way and moved off to the western margins of the plains.

As we said before, the Comanches were an offshoot of the mountain Shoshonis who came down into the plains when they got the horse. On the ground, they were an ungraceful people, being short-legged. But they were born riders. They transformed themselves into the showiest horsemen the world has ever seen. And in the way of born riders, they came to regard other people, both white and red, as inferior beings. This helped to make them immensely successful in war and in trade. In the 1600s there were perhaps 7,000 of them. That was considerably more than all the Apache families on the plains, and three times the number of their constant allies, the Kiowas.

The Kiowas were experts in sign language, the international language of the plains, by means of which the Plains Indians could talk very precisely. Here and there in other parts of the Indian world there was a language of hand signs too, but on the plains it was far more elaborate.

Perhaps this was connected with the fact that signals had been used on the plains since very ancient times: signals of smoke, fire, or signals made by waving blankets or by moving in a circle or back and forth. On the level high plains, where objects can be seen many miles away in the crystal-clear air, such signals would naturally develop. The first white men to enter the Southwest, in the 1540s, noted them. In later years the Sioux worked out a system of signaling with mirrors, and troops were often aware that Sioux were around them only by the flickering of light on distant bluffs and ridges. The Sioux were also said to have signaled at night with fire arrows. The United States and the British army adopted much of this signaling and used it—especially the heliograph—in the early days of the Signal Corps.

Living as they did near the Spanish settlements, some of the Kiowas and Comanches became prosperous traders. They occasionally livened things up by making early-summer raids on pueblos or settlements to collect captives and then brought them in to the great Taos trading fair to be ransomed. That made the Spanish officials furious. But they were careful not to offend the Comanches and in 1786 made a peace with them. They needed the Comanches to fight the Apaches. Besides, English trade goods were coming into the plains, and the Spaniards wanted all the trade-jobbers they could find to peddle their wares.

Comanche village in Texas, 1834. Buffalo hides covered tipis up to 25 feet in diameter.

The Taos trading fiesta, biggest doings in all the West, helped to hold the customers and keep them coming back. One of the most wanted items, oddly, was a large-sized silver cross. The Spanish missionaries offered them hopefully—and the Indians took them with gusto. The Comanches and Kiowas had no interest in the Christian religion, but they knew the crosses would fetch high prices on the plains. Hung around the necks of soldier-society chiefs, the crosses would be greatly admired as emblems of high rank. Horses were always the staple goods of trade. Some—probably the best-blooded—were bought from the Spanish settlements. Many more were stolen, particularly in raids on the Texas settlements. The Comanches and Kiowas would then go into winter camp on the upper Arkansas River with Cheyennes and Arapahoes, and do a thriving business in horses and other trade goods—including slaves, both red and white.

In 1821 a party of American traders camped at an enormous plains rendezvous like this. It had 700 lodges. And countless horses. For safety's sake the extra-fine ones were kept in the very center of the camp. But even there they weren't safe. Two days' journey away on the Platte River was a Crow camp. Nearly every night brave young Crows would creep into the center and steal some of the very finest horses right out of their log pens.

The Comanches got along very well with the Spanish and later on they wanted to get along with the Americans. After Texas won her independence from Mexico, the Indians several times asked for a formal peace. But each time they insisted on a definite boundary—they didn't want settlers encroaching on their territory. And this the

JAMES JEROME HILL REFERENCE LIBRA

Travelers in the Comanche country circled their wagons in a corral to fend off Indian attacks.

Texas politicians would not agree to. The way they felt about it, any Texas citizen could be settled on any land so long as it wasn't already occupied by a white owner. Indians must move away and keep away from the settlements, wherever they were.

So no peace was made. And in the spring of 1836 Kiowas and Nokoni Comanches swept down from the north on the settlement of Elder John Parker and his children and relatives, of whom there were some three dozen in all. The Indians killed several people and took five captives. The tales told by some of these captive women, after they were ransomed and returned, did much to make the name Comanche a byword for cruelty on the Texas frontier.

One of the captives, however, was not recovered for many years. This was Cynthia Ann Parker, who was a little girl at the time of her capture. She eventually became a wife of Nokoni, chief of the important Nokoni Comanches, and bore him several children. Her brother visited her "in her Indian home" after some years, but could not persuade her to return. Finally she was brought back to civilization by force, together with a baby. But both died soon afterward. A son named Quanah, about 15 at that time, stayed with his father, Nokoni, who had become the most important of Comanche leaders. After Nokoni died, Quanah, who was a person of great ability, rose to be head chief of the Comanches.

In 1839 Texas set aside more than $1,000,000 for military expenses. Citizen-soldier companies were formed and sometimes traveled hundreds of miles to find and attack Comanche rancherias.

In March 1840, a small band of Comanches was invited to a peace conference in the council house at San Antonio. There they were treacherously surrounded by troops and captured, several dozen Indians and a few militiamen being killed in the process. About a week later, Isomania, a very well-known Comanche leader, rode into town with a single companion. The chief lambasted the Texans for their treachery. Then he roared challenges to the troops to come out and fight the army of warriors he had left parked outside the town. The Texas citizen-soldiers didn't take up the challenge. They carefully explained to Isomania that there was a truce on at the moment. As usual, it was the scattered frontier settlers who suffered most from the vengeful young Indian warriors.

Officially, most of the Comanches kept peace with the United States—most of the time. But Texas was something else again. The Comanches did not recognize Texas as part of the United States, even when it was admitted as a state in 1845. After the San Antonio affair, the Comanches made a distinction between Texans and other Americans, and murderous raids on settlers and travelers along the Texas frontier became a regular part of Comanche life.

It was bad for the white men. But it was much worse for the Indians because, over the years, what all the raids and counter-raids led to was more and more poverty. Every time a village was destroyed, there went up in smoke not only the immediate food supply of dried meat and pemmican but the product of years of hunting and work as well. Buffalo robes, beaded clothes, thousands of arrows, tipis and their hard-to-get poles, handmade articles of all kinds, were burned by the museum-load. Horses, the real treasure, were stolen by the herd or killed on the spot, sometimes in vast numbers. After one raid on a Kiowa camp in the Texas Panhandle, 1,400 captured horses and mules are said to have been killed by a United States Army column. Early reports from the plains speak of the wealth and prosperity of the people. Later reports show how decade by decade the people grew poorer.

It was this long wearing down that at last broke the Plains Indians. In 1865 the Comanches and Kiowas signed a treaty with the United States. The treaty reserved for them the Panhandle of Texas and sundry other lands.

Texas, however, had other ideas about that. From the time it was a state, it had pleaded that the spread of settlement was "perfectly irresistible" and insisted on putting all the Indians out. So two years later the Comanches and Kiowas were persuaded to accept a revised treaty and were settled in Indian Territory. Shortly afterward it became clear what Texas meant by the "perfectly irresistible" spread of settlement. Chicago investors set up in the Texas Panhandle the largest single cattle ranch in the history of the West. This ranch, the XIT, was bigger than the state of Connecticut. Eight hundred miles of barbed-wire fencing were required to enclose this great domain.

Not all the Comanches and Kiowas went to live at the Indian agency. And not all of those who went there stayed there. One who was still there in 1869 was a not very important chief named Tochoway. His deeds have been forgotten, but for one brief moment he stepped into the limelight for a phrase that has gone down the years. It happened six weeks after Custer destroyed Black Kettle's camp at Washita. General Phil Sheridan, Custer's superior, was on tour to test the temper of the shaken tribes, and he paid a visit to the agency. Tochoway, introducing himself, said that he was a "good Indian." "The only good Indians I ever saw were dead," the General returned. It was by no means the first time this staunch frontier notion had been expressed. But here it was, extermination in a nutshell, and it had the support of high rank. The public took the phrase to its heart and made it part of the language.

Quanah Parker, who was getting to be the most influential of all Comanche chiefs, refused to sign the treaty of 1867. He remained on the buffalo plains but stayed in the part that was reserved for Indian use. In the 1870s, when buffalo-hide hunters invaded the Indian country by the hundreds, Quanah Parker's band and the Kwahadi Comanches made a desperate effort to drive them out. Hostilities began in 1874 and spread to five states. Troops immediately poured into the Indian country to put

SMITHSONIAN INSTITUTION, BUREAU OF AMERICAN ETHNOLOGY

Quanah Parker, Comanche leader.

down the hostiles, and a couple of years later Quanah Parker surrendered with his band. It was then that his real career, and a long and distinguished one, began. He devoted the rest of his life to saving the remnant of his people under the hardships of agency life.

As for the Kiowas, the first two men who signed the 1867 treaty were their principal chief, Setangya, and a noted orator, warrior, and patriot by the name of Satanta. Both men continued to lead raids into Texas and both were arrested for their part in one. Old Setangya wrenched off his manacles, taking the flesh of his hands with them, and attacked his guards until he was shot to death. He meant the act for suicide and sang his death song first.

Satanta was released. But when the Kiowas joined in the war against the invading buffalo hunters, he was put back in prison for life. Four years later he, too, killed himself in the Texas state prison.

It may be that these two deaths were meant to inspire the Kiowas with an iron will to survive under the iron conditions of agency life. At any rate, this was what the Kiowas thought.

SMITHSONIAN INSTITUTION, BUREAU OF AMERICAN ETHNOLOGY

Satanta, Kiowa warrior and patriot, as photographed about 1870.

33. NAVAHOS

The same period that saw so much trouble in Texas brought permanent peace to a people in Arizona and New Mexico. This was the Navaho people, who up to this time had been constantly warlike—at least by reputation.

In their country of magic mesas, vermilion cliffs, and painted deserts, the Navahos had long before created a unique society. Captives and immigrants had made them a mixed people, and this in turn had triggered a lusty growth. By 1860 they numbered perhaps 10,000 people, far more than all the other Apache tribes put together. Their language was the only inheritance they continued to have in common with their Apache brothers. But what with all the words from new tongues, even the language had changed.

At some time after the Spaniards came into the Southwest, the Navahos took to raising sheep. They became herdsmen and stockmen. Their women learned weaving and made the Navaho blanket world famous. Their men learned silversmithing. The silver work was so fine that Pueblo importers came to trade for it, bargaining in sign language.

The Navahos adopted the altars of the Pueblos—the much admired "sand paintings" that the Navahos have made their own. They took over also many religious ceremonies of the Pueblos. And yet, though religious feeling sifted into every nook and cranny of the Navaho way of life, in the main their religion was simply living the Right Way and entreating the world to behave the Right Way.

They farmed. Wherever a touch of moisture in the earth would let them, they had peach trees and corn patches, Hopi style. Their hogans—crude earth lodges—were gathered in family clusters, the houses of a mother and her married daughters. Otherwise the hogans stood anywhere, while the brush shelters of summer were as scattered as their flocks. They never formed villages.

It was the custom when someone in a house died to abandon it. Usually the people would not touch a dead body from fear of the dead and of witchcraft. They would not touch even the body of a slain enemy, and they never picked up the practice of scalping.

For a semi-wandering people, the Nava-

MUSEUM OF THE AMERICAN INDIAN, HEYE FOUNDATION

Navaho woman at her loom in Ganado, Arizona. The tribe's weaving has become world-famous.

MUSEUM FÜR VÖLKERKUNDE, BERLIN

Navahos, painted in 1853. The striped blankets gave way later to ones with more intricate pattern.

hos were uncommonly industrious. But work didn't weigh down their spirits. Wit, laughter, and practical jokes enlivened their gatherings. And they took great joy in raiding. However, in the matter of raiding it is possible that the Navahos were as much sinned against as sinning.

It is true that the Spaniards often pictured New Mexico as a martyr suffering for centuries from the Navahos, the "Lords of the Soil." And there is no doubt that Navaho raiders did remove much movable property, including children and women, from the Spaniards and the Pueblos. But there must have been some plunderers from the other side, too, to capture the thousands of Navaho and Apache women and children who were commonly the slaves of the New Mexican settlements.

There were endless complaints of Navaho raids and thefts. To settle these, the governor of New Mexico in 1849 marched a body of troops westward from the Rio Grande to the Navaho country and made a treaty. The Navahos had nothing like an authorized chief—each band was completely independent under a head man informally chosen. However, a local patriarch who was held in high esteem—one Narbona—came with several hundred of his followers to meet with the Americans.

Narbona explained that lawless men

were everywhere, and that "their utmost vigilance had not rendered it possible for the Chiefs and good men to apprehend the guilty, or to restrain the wicked." But he offered to do everything possible to make up for Navaho thefts, and began then and there by turning over 130 sheep and four or five horses and mules.

A treaty of "perpetual peace and friendship" was signed. But then a Mexican with the Americans demanded still another horse. The Navahos objected. The governor threatened. The Navahos wheeled their horses and "scampered off at the top of their speed," and the governor ordered his troops to fire on them. Six or seven Navahos didn't get out of range in time and were killed, including the 80-year-old Narbona. The rest of the Navahos, "three to four hundred, all mounted and armed, and their arms in their hands," fled without offering any resistance. In his report of the incident, a young army officer noted that the artillery "also threw in among them, very handsomely—much to their terror, when they were afar off, and thought they could with safety relax their flight—a couple of round shot. These people evidently gave signs of being tricky and unreliable."

This diplomacy did not stop Navaho marauding. So Fort Defiance was established in the Navaho country in 1851. After that there was reasonable quiet for seven years. Then war blew up—out of an argument between a Navaho sub-chief and an army officer's Negro slave. The Navahos made a massed attack on Fort Defiance, and violent death and disaster filled the country anew.

The government was busy with the Civil War and could not take care of the Navahos then. It was not until the winter of 1863 and 1864 that Colonel Kit Carson was sent to round them up and did so. In the Canyon de Chelly his troops cut down 2,000 to 3,000 peach trees. Among other plantings, they found one field of corn that took 300 men the better part of a day to destroy. Flocks and herds were seized and butchered. Most of the Navahos were starved into submission and removed to a reservation near Fort Sumner in eastern New Mexico, to be reformed from the incurable brigands everyone said they were. The idea was to turn them into peaceful farmers.

After four years of much Navaho misery, the idea was given up and the Navahos were allowed to return to their own country—or rather to a part of it. The government gave them 55,000 sheep and goats to put them back in business. They had a hard time getting started again. But in the main the tribe grew bigger year by year, sometimes prospered, and was at peace.

34. THE LAST ARROW

For the Apaches there was no peace. As late as 1866 an Arizona county was still offering $250 for each Apache scalp.

From earliest Spanish days the Apaches had a mad-dog hatred for the whites. More than anything else, probably, it was the constant kidnaping and enslavement of their women and children that roused this enmity. Two thousand Indian slaves were held by white people in New Mexico and Arizona in the year 1866—after 20 years of American rule. In Sonora and Chihuahua there were even more Apache slaves.

When the first Yankees appeared in their country, the Apaches approached them with friendship. The Indians thought the White-eyes, as they commonly called Americans, might prove to be allies against the Mexicans. But hostile incidents occurred very soon. Apaches with their wild-flying hair (flying because it was the custom to shampoo it every day), their raggle-taggle bands, their dusty brush-hut rancherias in the dusty brush, looked miserably primitive. There was not much about them, at a glance, to command respect.

And there was a great deal to create suspicion. They came and went so softly. They were often pleasant and talkative, but without quite saying anything. There was about them a sly, grinning watchfulness. They were some of the most watchful people who ever lived—and they needed to be, because for centuries they had played the part of dangerous big game for hunters with guns.

In 1837, a bounty boom year, a party of American trappers invited a band of Mimbres Apaches to a fiesta at the Santa Rita copper mines, in southwestern New Mexico, and then massacred the guests, procuring many scalps. The Mimbrenos had until then been friendly to Americans. After that they could not be trusted. The Santa Rita had to be abandoned for several years on this account.

Americans mining for gold in western New Mexico in the early 1850s were annoyed by an Apache who hung around their camp. He was an unusual Apache, a giant of a man, comically bowlegged. The miners tied him up and lashed his bull back to ribbons as a warning to keep away. He was an important man of the Mimbrenos, and was related by marriage to chiefs of the White Mountain and Chiricahua bands who lived next door west. His name was Mangas Coloradas (Red Sleeves). He was probably close to 60 years old at the time of his flogging, and he lived to be about 70. And for the rest of his life he warred against white men, Mexicans and White-eyes alike, without mercy.

In 1861 the Chiricahua people were not only friendly to Americans but were cutting wood for a stage station in Apache Pass. A hot-headed young lieutenant who was leading some troops in search of plunderers called the leading Chiricahua men to a conference in his tent, above which he flew a white flag of truce. During the conference he tried to make prisoners of the

General Crook's famous Apache scouts fought Apache bands that remained hostile and helped track down Geronimo. Their reward was to be packed off as prisoners to Florida.

1907

Chiricahuas. Their chief and several others got away, and a battle began. The troops withdrew from the pass after each side had executed its prisoners. The Chiricahua chief was named Cochise. He escaped from the tent, so they say, with three bullets in his body. For the next ten years he warred against white men without mercy.

Together, Mangas Coloradas and Cochise laid waste the white settlements, and spread hatred of Americans. At the opening of the Civil War, when garrisons were recalled from most of the forts in Arizona and New Mexico, Arizona was swept practically clean of whites by the Apaches.

General James H. Carleton came into New Mexico then with 3,000 California volunteers. He set about exterminating the Apaches. Sonora and Chihuahua helped; Pimas, Papagos and Maricopas were given guns and Americans to lead them; miners were encouraged to return and go on Apache-killing expeditions (all expenses paid); and troops, at a wartime high, were used to the full. California methods were adopted, which meant that anything was all right so long as Apaches were killed. Officials would not object if Apaches were coaxed to appear for "treaty" talks and were then shot—old Mangas Coloradas was one of the first to fall for this. He died in 1863.

Some officials, such as Kit Carson and Colonel John C. Cremony, who had known the Apaches for years, simply ignored the orders to kill all men and take the women and children prisoner. They accepted Apache surrenders. But in general the forces went to their work with enthusiasm.

This is the image of the Indian warrior that lives on. Here he is, complete with war whoop and enemy scalp, in a painting made in 1907.

The war lasted almost ten years. The Apaches were driven deep into their mountains. But no Apache band was conquered.

As bitterness and cruelty went to new highs, hair-raising tales of Apache torture were told. We do not have, of course, the tales of white atrocities that Apaches may have told each other. But we do know that in the 1860s Arizona had the reputation of being the toughest territory in the West, filled with men who had got there a quick jump ahead of vigilantes. There is no reason to suppose they dealt gently with an Apache when they could get hold of one. In 1871 a Tucson mob massacred some 85 Apache people who had put themselves under the protection of the military at nearby Camp Grant. The outrage aroused indignation throughout the nation. But the Arizona papers defended the massacre. One hundred people were tried for it. After deliberating less than half an hour, a jury declared them not guilty.

"How is it?" asked Cochise, chief of the Chiricahuas. "Why is it that the Apaches want to die—that they carry their lives on their fingernails?"

The Camp Grant massacre ended the war of Apache extermination—a war that cost 1,000 American lives and more than 40 million dollars and achieved nothing. Things were admitted to be back where they were when the war started.

So now it was decided to try winning the Apaches over.

The frontier was seething with resentment. It was lucky that the command of the military department of Arizona was given in that summer of 1871 to General George Crook. He was an Indian fighter of skill and wisdom. What is more, he was stubbornly honest, a man who kept his word. He realized that the Apaches were not the devils they were said to be. They were frightened people who had become masters of guerrilla warfare because of their long experience as subjects of extermination.

The Apache could cover 40 miles in a day on foot, or could reel off 75 miles a day on horseback. He didn't care if he ran his horse into the ground—he could steal another at the nearest ranch. He could live off the country while his white pursuer was perishing of hunger, thirst, and sunstroke. He could travel as invisibly as a ghost, appear or disappear as silently as a shadow. The soldier on his trail knew of his presence only when a deadly Apache bow or rifle announced itself from a concealed and highly defendable position.

The dusty warrior, with a dash of color at the headband or in the Pima-like turban, was seldom seen, and if seen was seldom hit, and if hit was seldom knocked down to stay. Apaches were terribly hard to kill.

Crook employed warriors of Apache bands that had been won over to fight the bands that insisted on remaining hostile. His Apache scouts became famous, and by the end of summer, 1874, all important hostile bands had been either won over or rounded up and were settled on reservations. They were peaceful and were reported to be happy. There was "almost a certainty," said the governor of Arizona in 1875, "that no general Indian war will ever occur again."

The governor was over-optimistic.

The greatest cause of later trouble, among the Apaches, was the moving of bands from their homeland reservations to new reservations where they did not want to go. Sometimes the Indian Bureau did this for reasons of efficiency. Sometimes it removed Indians to throw the business of an agency to some go-getting community that was pulling strings to get it. Or for some similiar motives. The second greatest cause was the activity of crooked "rings" that claimed to provide supplies Indians never received, stole reservation land, or practiced other such arts and crafts. Captain Bourke, who was General Crook's adjutant for many years, said that the agent issued supplies by throwing them through the rungs of a ladder—the Indians got whatever stuck to the rungs, and the agent got what fell to the ground.

General Crook had something to say about this too. He had never seen an Indian so bad, he said, "that he was not an example in honor and nobility compared to the wretches who plunder him of the little our government appropriated for him."

Many Apache bands broke out in furious protests against such treatment, and the Chiricahuas most of all. The great Cochise died in peace on the Chiricahua reservation in 1874. But within 18 months some of the Chiricahuas were rampaging into Sonora, killing innocent bystanders all along the way. The Apaches did not want to be removed to another reservation.

For a good part of the next ten years Apaches broke loose to storm up and down the border country. Such leaders as Victorio and Geronimo (pronounced Heronimo) became top celebrities of the West. After Victorio was killed by Mexican troops in 1880, a rheumatic old gentleman named Nana stepped up front. For a couple of wild, unbelievable months in 1881 he led a handful of warriors on the champion raid-and-running campaign of them all. He

Geronimo. He began hating whites when his mother, wife, and children were massacred.

NATIONAL ARCHIVES

fought and won a battle a week against 1,000 United States troops, Texas Rangers, armies of civilians, and the military and police of northern Mexico. Nana was some 70 or 80 years old at the time and had to walk with a cane.

General Crook had been sent away to fight the Sioux in 1875, when Arizona was quiet and there was never again going to be an Indian war. He was brought back in 1882. For four years he patiently rounded up hostile Apaches and then patiently tried to pacify hostile people on the home front. He had to round up his Apaches again and again when they were prodded into other outbreaks. Geronimo came to the front in this period and made his name a matter of dread on both sides of the border.

There came a time when Crook's superiors grew tired of hearing him insist on honorable behavior. They put General Nelson A. Miles in his place. When Apache scouts were able to talk Geronimo into surrendering again, he and his band were packed off to Florida as prisoners. And for good measure, Miles sent along Crook's old Apache scouts as prisoners too. And just to make sure he had everyone, he sent along all the other Chiricahuas he could lay hands on, including hundreds who had remained quietly on the reservations from the first.

This happened in 1886. In 1890 Crook was still trying to get Congress to get his Apaches moved back west when he died of a heart attack. A few months before his death he visited the largest group of exiled Chiricahuas, who had been settled for the time being in Mount Vernon Barracks, near Mobile, Alabama. They crowded around him, his old scouts and his ancient enemies, and there was quite a reunion. And this is as good a place as any other to declare a final, formal end of the Indian wars.

Painting of an Apache made in 1828.

35. RESERVATIONS

From end to end of the two continents the American Indians lived, and they still do. By about 1900, the Indian people in the United States had shrunk to 250,000, or less than one-third the number estimated to have been in this area before Columbus. Since 1900 the figure has doubled. The Vanishing Americans are increasing at a rate faster than the rest of the population, and by 1975 it is expected there will be 700,000. Canada has more than 160,000 Indians.

But we have to remember that all this area north of Mexico was just the fringe of the central Indian world. In Latin America there are still more than 29,000,000 who regard themselves as Indian. In the United States, however, the Indians form less than one-half of one per cent of the total population, while in Colombia, Bolivia, Peru, and Guatemala they make up to 40 to 50 per cent and even more. Many more millions are of mixed blood.

In some ways the Indian story in the rest of the hemisphere has been like the story in the United States. Indian lands were broken up, Indians were transformed into peons, wars of resistance were fought. But in Latin America generally, Indian culture mingled with European and, in regions where there had been heavy Negro slavery, with African. In this mingling, certain Indian traits have remained, and the people are proud of them. Today Latin Americans tend to glorify Indian history and individual Indians, such as Juarez, who was elected President of Mexico in 1861. In Mexico, Indian feeling is strongest and has had a great influence on art.

"Indianism" has led to a change in policy toward Indians in various American countries. Brazil in 1910 founded the Service for the Protection of the Indian, to bring education and modern medicine and agriculture to the many tribes of Amazonia, and to make these tribes a part of national life. Thirty years later, 19 American republics organized the Inter-American Indian Institute. It has done much good work. Its attitude is that the Indian tribe or community should be encouraged rather than broken up.

In the United States the attitude for many years was the exact opposite of this. Here many things complicated the problem, and especially the fact that most tribes still owned some property which various citizens never gave up trying to get.

In the Indians' darkest hour—the 1870s to the 1920s—there was, no doubt, much more silent suffering than will ever be told. Hunger was the big reality. But there was much else. Religious activities were forbidden. Children were taught to feel ashamed of their "blanket Indian" parents and of all their ways. For many agency Indians life was made aimless and hopeless by the concentration-camp atmosphere. Thousands of spiritless people merely killed time.

GRAND RAPIDS PUBLIC LIBRARY

On November 4, 1886 these ragged frightened Apache children arrived at the Carlisle, Pennsylvania, Indian School to be educated.

GRAND RAPIDS PUBLIC LIBRARY

A photograph of the same Apache children four months later—scrubbed, barbered, and dressed in the academy's neat uniforms.

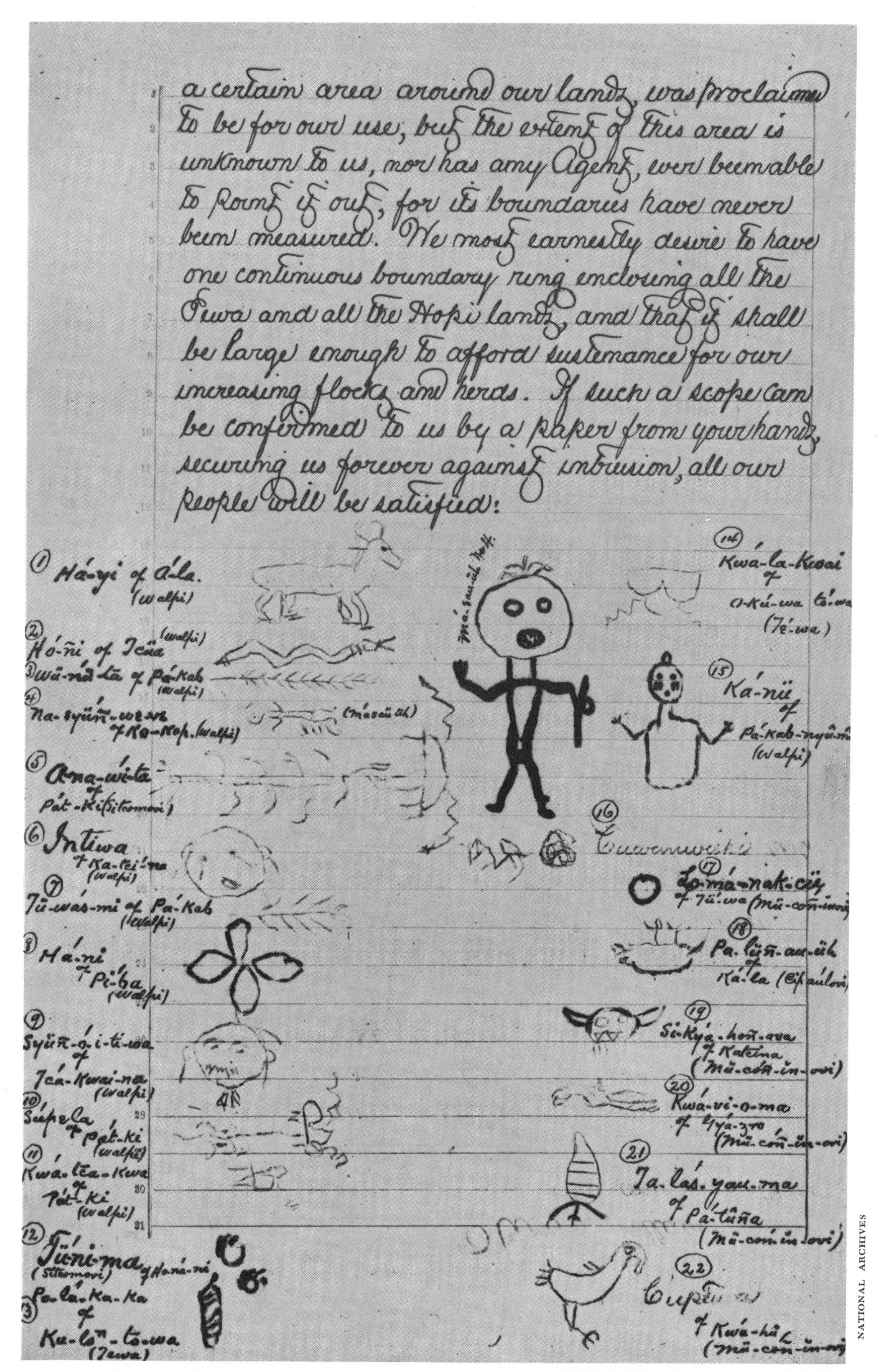

a certain area around our lands, was proclaimed to be for our use; but the extent of this area is unknown to us, nor has any Agent, ever been able to point it out, for its boundaries have never been measured. We most earnestly desire to have one continuous boundary ring enclosing all the Tewa and all the Hopi lands, and that it shall be large enough to afford sustenance for our increasing flocks and herds. If such a scope can be confirmed to us by a paper from your hands, securing us forever against intrusion, all our people will be satisfied:

This last page of a Hopi petition (1894) is signed with the totem symbols of their leaders.

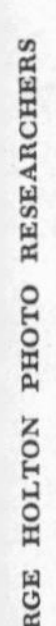

The Spaniards taught this Peruvian to wear the hat he holds. The cap and poncho are Inca.

Reservation lands were supposed to belong to the Indians forever. But as land in the West picked up in value, the reservations began to look bigger to the white men every day. So in 1887 the Allotment Act was passed. It was designed to make all Indians and their problems disappear—and to put the broad reservations in the hands of white owners. Under this law, tribes were to give up their reservations. Bits of them would be allotted to individual Indians as small, family-sized farms. And the immense amount of land left over was to be declared "surplus." A token payment would be paid to the tribes for this "surplus," and then it was to be opened to white ownership.

Many sincere friends of the Indians believed in the Act. They believed it would change all Indians into industrious small farmers just like anybody else, thought this was a good thing, and backed the measure. Even General Crook helped to get the plains tribes to go through the motions of accepting it. And more than 100 reservations were allotted.

So far as the real-estate business was concerned, the Act succeeded magnificently. Of the 150 million acres owned by the Indians in 1880, over 90 million acres—an area more than twice the size of Oklahoma—were taken back from the Indians.

As for civilizing the Indians, which was supposed to be the aim of the Allotment Act, that was a failure. Allottees did not turn instantly into sturdy small farmers. In many cases it wouldn't have helped much if they had. For even the sturdiest immigrant peasants from Europe went gaunt trying to work small claims in northern plains. Instead, by one means or another, the Indians lost their farms, and hundreds of families became paupers.

Clearly the Allotment Act had been a mistake. So in 1934 the Indian Reorganization Act was passed. It put a stop to any more allotting of tribal lands and tried to get back for the Indians any of the "surplus" reservation lands that had not yet been homesteaded. It tried to help the Indians get on their feet by encouraging group spirit.

A surprising amount of group spirit had survived all the attempts to break up the tribes. When government representatives went out and talked to the tribes and bands and offered them loan funds for constructive community purposes, most Indian groups jumped at the offers. For the first time in history Indian lands were increased. Tribe after tribe pulled itself up by its bootstraps. With the help of the new law, thousands of Indian families were restored to a life of some hope and independence. More Indians began to attend public schools. And before long an educated Indian was no longer a rare thing. Indian college students were no longer uncommon.

Native languages, crafts, ceremonies, traditions were not only permitted, they were promoted. Venerable medicine men journeyed hundreds of miles in almost equally venerable cars or pickup trucks to teach the correct rituals to young people living in towns. Factory workers came home from Detroit or San Francisco to take part in the Sun Dance or the Corn Dance.

By and large the people were still very poor but there was a difference. Most communities made an astonishing quick climb. The tribes, those that were left, showed that they still had a power to help themselves if they were encouraged to use it.

In World War II, about 25,000 Indians

HARVEY CAPLIN

A Ute Indian in full feathered ceremonial dress, ready to perform an ancient dance.

MILTON SNOW, U.S. INDIAN SERVICE

These Hopi garden plots show on what a small scale these Indians carry on desert farming.

At the right is a recent photograph of Apaches ceremoniously dressed for the Mountain Spirit Dance. Indians are proud of their traditions, and their dances have deep meaning for them.

This is not a scarecrow. In a tobacco patch, still sacred to his people, an Iroquois of Ontario continues the tradition of wearing a false face mask.

PETER GREENE, PHOTO RESEARCHERS

MILTON SNOW, NAVAHO SERVICE

Navahos meet at Window Rock, Arizona, to discuss tribal affairs. With a population of 80,000, the Navahos are the giants of the present-day Indian world.

served in the armed forces. During their service some of them really learned English for the first time, and thousands had their first real look at the outside world and went back home full of new notions for their families and the tribal communities.

But in 1950 the government's Indian policy changed again. Once more efforts were made to take away Indian land and to chop back or break down the tribal societies. A program was started to end all federal help and get the government out of the Indian business.

In 1960 a group of experts, sponsored by the University of Chicago, began an inquiry into Indian matters today. The following summer they invited the National Congress of American Indians, an organization of some 80 member tribes, to a conference in Chicago. Other Indian spokesmen were invited also. They were all to help by giving the points of view of the Indian people. What did they want? What future did they envision for themselves? How should the government help?

In this last generation the number of Indian men and women in the professions, both in and out of the Indian world, has increased greatly. Movement back and forth from the Indian to the white world has become much freer. At the same time the idea that sooner or later Indians would become totally absorbed has steadily lost ground. Most experts feel that Indian tribes and communities will keep their separate character for a long, long time into the future. Most experts believe this is good, not bad.

Most Indians today are still very poor,

their health is poor, and the general level of education is poor. Some groups, though, taken altogether, still own considerable property. People who, in the old frontier phrase, have more gall than character, are still trying to get it away from them and sometimes do. But more and more organizations and persons are watching out for the Indians' interests.

Those Indians who live on reservations or on restricted trust land do not pay taxes on the land or the income from it. Those on the rolls of the Bureau of Indian Affairs are in most matters under federal jurisdiction. In these respects Indians are "wards" of the United States. The term means protection: The United States, in return for value received, has guaranteed to protect various Indian peoples from local acts—acts such as drove out the Five Civilized Tribes. For good reasons, most Indians feel they need this protection.

In all other ways Indians are full-fledged citizens. Some 50,000 are citizens of their home states. Among these are more than 7,500 Six Nations Iroquois in New York. Modern Mohawks have made something of a national reputation as structural steel workers.

Indian Territory fell under the axe of the Allotment Act and became Oklahoma in 1907. That brought to an end the long, hopeless fight of the Five Civilized Tribes to keep the territory they had been promised would be theirs as long as water kept on running. Ever since they got there, pieces of their land had been repeatedly taken away for other groups of displaced Indians or for white settlement. The 75,000 Cherokees of Oklahoma are still by far the largest of the many Indian groups in the state and one of the largest in the

CENTRAL LIBRARY DEPARTMENT OF THE INTERIOR

Pueblo artist Maria Martinez at work on her famous pottery.

THOMAS HOLLYMAN, PHOTO RESEARCHERS

A Chocó hunter in a Colombian forest.

MAKAH
QUILEUTE
HOH
QUINAULT
SHOALWATER
LUMMI
SWINOMISH
SNOHOMISH
SALISH
CHEHALIS
WASHINGTON
COLVILLE
SPOKANE
KALISPEL
KOOTENAI
BLACKFEET
ASSINIBOINE
YAKIMA
GRAND RONDE
SILETZ
COLUMBIA RIVER
COEUR D'ALENE
SALISH
FLATHEAD
KOOTENAI
CHIPPEWA
CREE
ATSINA
SIOUX
ASSINIBOINE
CHIPPEWA
ARIKARA
GROS VENTRE
MANDAN
SIOUX
CAYUSE
WALLA WALLA
WALLA WALLA
WASCO
NEZ PERCE
SNAKE RIVER
MONTANA
YELLOWSTONE RIVER
NORTH DAKOTA
OREGON
KLAMATH
SNAKE
PAIUTE
MODOC
CROW
CHEYENNE
SIOUX
IDAHO
SHOSHONE
ARAPAHO
SHOSHONE
WYOMING
HOOPA
YUROK
PAIUTE
PIT RIVER
PAIUTE
PAIUTE
SHOSHONE
BANNOCK
SIOUX
WAILAKI
MAIDU
MAIDU
SHOSHONE
PAIUTE
SHOSHONE
SHOSHONE
SHOSHONE
PAIUTE
WASHOE
POMO
SHOSHONE
GREAT SALT LAKE
NEBRASKA
PAIUTE
GOSIUTE
WASHOE
PAIUTE
SHOSHONE
PAIUTE
GOSIUTE
UTE
PLATTE RIVER
ME-WUK
SHOSHONE
MONO
PAIUTE
NEVADA
UTAH
COLORADO
CHUKCHANSI
PAIUTE
PAIUTE
PAIUTE
PAIUTE
COLORADO RIVER
UTE
UTE
TULE RIVER
PAIUTE
HAVASUPAI
NAVAHO
ARKANSAS RIVER
CALIFORNIA
HOPI
APACHE
HUALAPAI
PUEBLOS
MOHAVE
ARIZONA
CHEMEHUEVI
NAVAHO
YAVAPAI
MOHAVE-APACHE
ZUÑI
PUEBLOS
CANADIAN
MISSION
MOHAVE
MOHAVE-APACHE
NAVAHO
NEW MEXICO
PIMA
MARICOPA
RED RIVER
YUMA
PACIFIC OCEAN
COCOPAH
PAPAGO
APACHE
APACHE
PAPAGO
TEXAS
RIO GRANDE
KANSAS
QUAPAW MIAMI MODOC
PEORIA OTTAWA SHAWNEE
SENECA CAYUGA
WYANDOTTE
KAW
OKLAHOMA
TONKAWA
PONCA
PAWNEE
MISSOURI OTOE
CHEROKEE
SAUK AND FOXES
CHEYENNE
ARAPAHO
IOWA
CREEKS
KICKAPOO
ARKANSAS RIVER
SHAWNEE
POTAWATOMI
SEMINOLE
CADDO
DELAWARES
WICHITA
KIOWA
COMANCHE
CHOCTAW
KIOWA-APACHE
CHICKASAW
TEXAS
RED RIVER
SCALE 0 25 50 75 MILES
SCALE
0 50 100 150 MILES

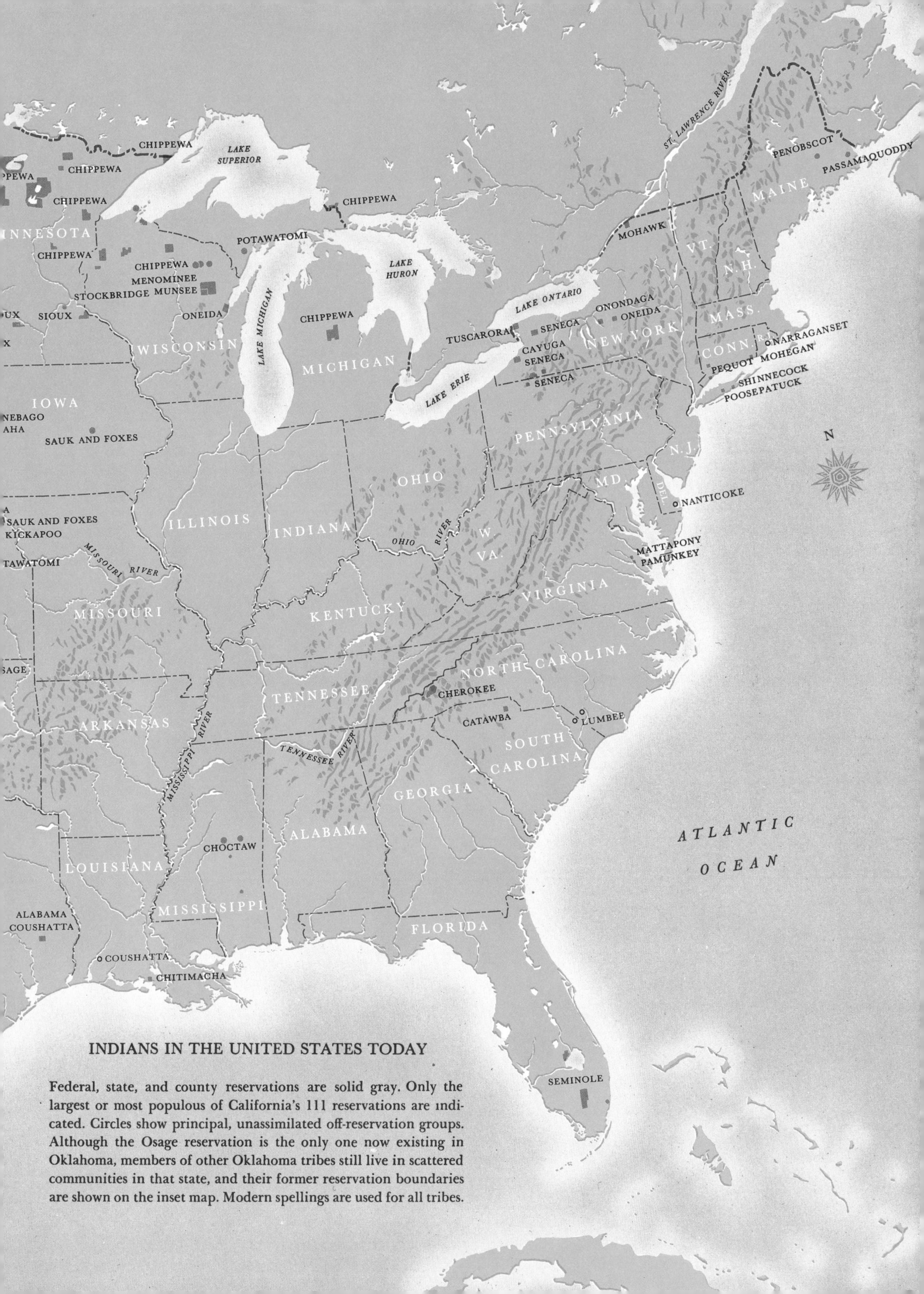

INDIANS IN THE UNITED STATES TODAY

Federal, state, and county reservations are solid gray. Only the largest or most populous of California's 111 reservations are indicated. Circles show principal, unassimilated off-reservation groups. Although the Osage reservation is the only one now existing in Oklahoma, members of other Oklahoma tribes still live in scattered communities in that state, and their former reservation boundaries are shown on the inset map. Modern spellings are used for all tribes.

ALVIN M. JOSEPHY

country. The state also counts 40,000 Choctaws, 20,000 Creeks, 9,000 Chickasaws, and 3,000 Seminoles.

The Osages used to be the wealthiest of the tribes—oil was discovered on their reservation in eastern Oklahoma. Some Quapaws, owners of lead and zinc finds in their corner of Indian Territory, once ran the Osages a close second as richest Indians. Today the title goes to the tiny Agua Caliente band in California, 100 persons, who own much of the real estate in the resort town of Palm Springs. In 1958 their per capita assets were rated at $339,577. The title for the poorest went at the same time to the Sisseton Sioux of South Dakota, with per capita assets of $19.12.

The Navahos, with a 15-million-acre reservation and 80,000 people, are the giants of the present-day Indian world in the United States. Their tribal budget for 1958 was more than $15,000,000. One-third of it went for the tribal scholarship fund.

Fighting men have come and gone, but the people of peace, the Hopis, are still in their country. The peaceful Pimas are still along the Gila. The great Spanish empire has long since vanished, but Zuni, so easily conquered on that July day centuries ago, is still very real and very present.

Tourists by the thousands visit the Hopi towns, Zuni, and other Pueblo villages. They find there a value clear apart from all the earnest matters discussed in these last pages, a value that may be one of the most important of all the American Indian's contributions. It is a sense of permanence, the sense of an infinite past that implies an infinite future. The thought is comforting, and one for which the world seems hungry. It is good to feel that the history of the American Indian, any more than the history of America, is not finished.

Among these children in a regular public school at Nespelem, Wash., are descendants of Chief Joseph's Nez Perce warriors. Indians cooperate instead of competing. Thus children often try not to "appear better" than others.

ACKNOWLEDGMENTS

The Editors are grateful to many individuals and organizations for their generous assistance and counsel in the preparation of this book. Space does not allow the listing of all of them, but special acknowledgment is due to D'Arcy McNickle, Frederick J. Dockstader, Director of the Museum of the American Indian, Heye Foundation, New York, and to the following:

Alabama Department of Archives and History, Montgomery: Peter A. Brannon
American Museum of Natural History, New York: Harry Shapiro, Junius Bird, Gordon Ekholm, Robert Elwood Logan
Bancroft Library, University of California, Berkeley: George B. Hammond, J. S. Holliday, Robert H. Becker, Dale L. Morgan, John Barr Tompkins
Marius Barbeau, Ottawa
Mark F. Boyd, Tallahassee, Florida
British Museum, London: P. B. C. Bridgewater, A. C. Gray
Ernest Brown Collection, Edmonton, Alberta: Gladys Reeves
John Carter Brown Library, Providence, Rhode Island: Thomas R. Adams
Chicago Natural History Museum: E. Leland Webber, John S. Martin
Detroit Public Library, Burton Historical Collection: James T. Babcock
Edward Eberstadt & Sons, New York: Charles and Lindley Eberstadt
James L. Giddings, Jr., Brown University, Providence, Rhode Island
Gilcrease Institute, Tulsa, Oklahoma: Dean Krakel, Glen Ames, David R. Milsten, Charles Proctor, Bruce Wear, Martin Wenger
Glenbow Foundation, Calgary, Alberta: Hugh Dempsey, Mrs. Eleanor Ediger
Grand Rapids Public Library, Grand Rapids, Michigan: Esther M. Tracey
Hudson's Bay Company, London and Winnipeg
Henry E. Huntington Library and Art Gallery, San Marino, California: Robert O. Dougan, Carey Bliss, Mary Isabel Fry, Haidee Noya, John E. Pomfret, Lyle H. Wright
James Jerome Hill Reference Library, St. Paul, Minnesota: Russell F. Barnes, Anna M. Heilmaier
Library of Congress, Washington, D.C.: Edgar Breitenbach, Howard F. Cline, Milton Kaplan
Tony Linck
Museo Naval, Madrid: Capitan Julio F. Guillen
Museum für Völkerkunde, Berlin: H. Hartmann
Museum für Völkerkunde, Vienna: Etta Becker-Donner, Karl A. Nowotny
Museum of History and Industry
National Archives, Washington: Wayne C. Grover, Robert Bahmer, Herman R. Friis, Carmelita Ryan, Forest L. Williams
National Gallery of Canada, Ottawa: Kathleen M. Fenwick
National Museum of Canada, Ottawa: Harold Pfeiffer, Katherine Bowlby, Audrey E. Dawe
National Park Service, Department of the Interior, Washington, D.C.: Carroll A. Burroughs, the late James J. Cullinane, Virginia Daiker, John W. Griffin, Herbert Kahler
New-York Historical Society: James J. Heslin, Betty J. Ezequelle
New York Public Library: Lewis M. Stark, Mrs. Maud Cole, Mrs. Philomena Houlihan, Elizabeth E. Roth
New York State Museum, Albany: William N. Fenton, Charles Gillette
Oakland Art Museum: Paul Mills, Mrs. I. M. Heyman
Peabody Museum of Archaeology and Ethnology, Harvard University: Mrs. Katherine B. Edsall
Philbrook Art Center, Tulsa, Oklahoma: Victor Hurt, Mrs. Jeanne Snodgrass
Provincial Museum, Victoria: G. Clifford Carl, Wilson Duff
Public Archives of Canada, Ottawa: W. Kaye Lamb, Pierre Brunet, Georges Delisle
Royal Ontario Museum, Toronto; Canadiana Collections
Seattle Art Museum; Richard Fuller, Mrs. Joan Fechter
Smithsonian Institution, Washington: John C. Ewers, Mrs. Margaret C. Blaker, Robert Elder, Edgar M. Howell, Sol H. Reisenberg, William C. Sturtevant
Southwest Museum, Los Angeles: Carl S. Dentzel, Mrs. Charles Amsden, Mrs. Ella L. Robinson, Charles Rozaire, Ruth D. Simpson
University Museum, University of Pennsylvania
Utah State Historical Society, Salt Lake City: A. R. Mortensen, John James, Jr., Mrs. Margaret Sheperd
Victor W. Von Hagen, Lima, Peru
Washington State Historical Society, Tacoma: Bruce Le Roy
Wisconsin State Historical Society, Madison: Paul Vanderbilt, Cheryle M. Hughes
Yale University Library: Western Americana Collection: Archibald Hanna
William Zimmerman, Washington

Index

Landmark
Giant